CULTURES OF THE WORLD

COLOMBIA

Jill DuBois

MARSHALL CAVENDISH
New York • London • Sydney

Reference edition published 1993 by
Marshall Cavendish Corporation
2415 Jerusalem Avenue
P.O. Box 587
North Bellmore
New York 11710

© Times Editions Pte Ltd 1991

Originated and designed by
Times Books International, an imprint of
Times Editions Pte Ltd

Printed in Singapore

Library of Congress Cataloging-in-Publication Data:
DuBois, Jill, 1952–
    Colombia / Jill DuBois.
      p. cm.—(Cultures Of The World)
    Includes bibliographical references and index.
    Summary: Introduces the geography, culture,
    and lifestyles of Colombia.
    ISBN 1-85435-384-5
    1. Colombia. [1. Colombia.] I. Title. II. Series.
F2258.5.D83 1991
986.1—dc20   90–22468
           CIP
           AC

Cultures of the World

Editorial Director	Shirley Hew
Managing Editor	Shova Loh
Editors	Roseline Lum
	Siow Peng Han
	Leonard Lau
	MaryLee Knowlton
Picture Editor	Jane Duff
Production	Edmund Lam
Design	Tuck Loong
	Lee Woon Hong
	Dani Phoa
	Ong Su Ping
	Katherine Tan
Illustrator	Thomas Koh

INTRODUCTION

COLOMBIA lies in an area of geological instability that makes it prone to earthquakes and volcanic eruptions. And these days its volatile nature extends to political and social conditions as well. Thus few people know much about this South American country beyond what they read in the newspaper headlines.

Yet Colombia is a land of rich traditions, beautiful and historic cities, and scenic countryside. With half the territory being inaccessible and uninhabitable, the Colombians have always had to possess an indomitable spirit to make it possible for their country to maintain its position as a leader among the Latin American nations.

As part of the series *Cultures of the World,* this book will familiarize you with the attitudes, lifestyles and artistic passion of the people who live, work and play in the country that many call "the Athens of Latin America."

BOGOTÁ

CONTENTS

Dancing, as depicted on the wall of this restaurant, is a feature of life on the Caribbean coast.

CONTENTS

All manner of transport is used to move produce and people to the market place in rural areas.

GEOGRAPHY

COLOMBIA IS THE ONLY COUNTRY in Latin America named for Christopher Columbus, who "discovered" the Americas. Located in the northwestern part of the continent, its neighboring countries are Panama to the north, Venezuela and Brazil to the east, and Peru and Ecuador to the south. It is the only South American country with coasts on both the Caribbean Sea and the Pacific Ocean.

Colombia is the fourth largest state in South America, with a surface area of 440,000 square miles, which is approximately the size of Texas, Oklahoma and New Mexico combined. Eight islands are also under Colombian rule. They are Gorgona, Gorgonilla and Malpelo in the Pacific Ocean; and San Andrés, Providencia, San Bernardo, Islas del Rosario and Isla Fuerte in the Caribbean Sea.

Left: **The Tairona National Park is an untouched jungle at the foot of the Sierra Nevada de Santa Marta, a mountain that drops abruptly into the Caribbean Sea.**

Opposite: **At this point called Pastos Knot, the Andean range opens into the three *cordilleras* which run down the whole length of the country.**

The Cordillera Occidental is the lowest and the least populated of the three mountain ranges. It blocks the Cauca valley from the Pacific coast.

TOPOGRAPHY

The distinguishing feature of Colombia is the Andean mountain chain in the central and western parts of the country. The *cordilleras* divide the country down its length. Cordillera Oriental (Eastern Range) is the longest, the highest is the massive Cordillera Central, and Cordillera Occidental (Western Range) is close to the frontier with Ecuador. Snow covers the summits of the Central and Eastern ranges, which also have volcanoes. The country is also divided by river systems and climate differences.

The river basins between the mountain ranges contain Colombia's three most important rivers: the Atrato, the Sinú and the Magdalena. The Magdalena, the "lifeline of Colombia," flows northward between the Central and Eastern ranges and empties into the Caribbean. Though it is full of falls, sandbars, eddies and sunken rocks, it is channeled so that large vessels can travel as far as Barranquilla on the northern Caribbean coastline. The other two great rivers are the Amazon and the Orinoco. The latter forms a boundary between Colombia and Venezuela.

Colombia is a land of many contrasts. Besides desert wastelands, such as the Guajira Desert featured here, one can find rainforests, temperate valleys, cold windswept plains and snow-capped mountains.

CLIMATE

Mountain ranges make up 45% of the land surface; and in these ranges, there are high plateaus and cool valleys. Because Colombia is situated on the equator, the climate of the various regions is determined mainly by altitude. The coastal and eastern plains, known as *los llanos*, are at low altitudes. Thus they benefit from a tropical climate. The temperate regions, located in the northernmost section of the Andes mountain chain, are mostly agricultural. These regions have annual temperatures of 65° to 70°. Small coffee plantations are located on the craggy hillsides, with houses propped up in the less tillable areas. The cold regions, situated between 6,000 and 9,000 feet above sea level, have an average temperature of 53°. Above 9,000 feet, the severely cold regions have temperatures that go down below 50°. This land can only be used for grazing. The snow line begins at about 15,000 feet.

The two coasts of Colombia vary greatly in the amount of rainfall each receives. Guajira, at the northern tip of the country, is the driest place in Colombia, with an average yearly rainfall of only 10 inches. On the other hand, cities in Chocó department on the Pacific coast have average yearly rainfall of nearly 400 inches. (In Colombia, states are called departments.)

9

Right: **The toucan, with its characteristic bill, is one of the many species of birds that can be found in Colombia.**

Below: **The cute *irara* makes its home in the Amazon forest.**

FAUNA

Many exotic animals thrive in the tropical climate of Colombia, including crocodiles, tapirs, ocelots and armadillos. Several types of monkeys are also found in large numbers in the tropical forests. In addition, there are many birds with bright and colorful plumage living in Colombia. Among these are macaws, parrots, jacamars, cotingas and toucans. There are about 1,500 species of birds, ranging from the tiny hummingbird to the large harpy eagle which eats sloths, monkeys, opossums and guinea pigs. The graceful condor which hovers over the mountain slopes also lives in this country.

The rivers of Colombia and their tributaries contain freshwater species of fish usually found in the open sea, including dolphins and stingrays. The fish vary greatly in size, from the tiny guppy and neon tetra to the arapaima, which is one of the largest freshwater fish in the world. Colombia's waters are also home to dangerous piranhas which travel in large schools.

FLORA

More than 4,000 species of plants, including 700 varieties of orchids, grow in Colombia. The many types of climates make it possible for a diversity of flora to grow in the country. In the northern deserts, cactus and agaves can grow as tall as 60 feet. In the center of the country, the *llanos* expanse, there are vast wooded areas with a great wealth of flora. The humidity allows the cultivation of olive trees.

Very few plants can stand the cold winds that sweep across the *páramos*. One of them is the silvery *espeletias*.

Orchids with large, vividly-colored flowers form a lush undergrowth in the Amazonian forest of dense trees. Tropical plants yield rubber, chicle, vanilla, sarsaparilla and ginger, and medical products such as ipecac, quinine and castor beans. Exotic fruits, including papayas, mangoes, melons, pineapples, passion fruit, bananas and coconuts come from this region. Others, virtually unknown in the United States, like the *curuba, chirimoya, guanbana, zapote, granadilla* and *pitahaya*, are also grown in Colombia.

Colombia's many mountains are covered with forests of pine, oak and other trees. These more temperate regions produce flowers such as roses, chrysanthemums and hortensia, which bloom throughout the year. Coffee plantations are also located here, and various small trees are planted to shade the coffee bushes. Eucalyptus, originally imported from Australia, grows well in this region.

The windy, cold *páramos* or high plains of the *tierra fría* are covered with low vegetation of vine shrubs, mosses and resinous woody plants.

The Cauca River winds its way smoothly through the emerald-green sugar-cane fields. Thanks to its many rivers, Colombia can supplement much of its energy requirements with hydroelectricity.

MINERAL WEALTH

Mineral wealth abounds in Colombia. It is the world's major source of emeralds. In addition, it ranks fifth in the world in platinum production and ninth in gold. Other significant reserves include petroleum and natural gas, coal, silver, copper, lead, iron, mercury, nickel and uranium.

Colombia is also beginning to benefit from one of its most undeveloped regions, the Guajira peninsula, located on the northeast corner of the Caribbean coast. Poor agricultural conditions have prevented the area from being cultivated, though there has been an active salt mine there for years. Recently, however, geologists have discovered that the peninsula is rich in mineral deposits. Natural gas, coal and limestone have turned a desert into an economic success. The Guajira fields are currently producing more than 80% of the natural gas utilized in the country's northern coast.

Because of its mountains and rivers, Colombia is one of the greatest producers of hydroelectricity in Latin America. But, although an ambitious program of hydropower development is under way, supply has fallen short of demand.

A TOWN FLOODED WITH TROUBLES

It was a quiet night in the central Colombian town of Armero, and most of the 22,000 residents were asleep when the downpour began. But it was not rain that was falling. Instead it was volcanic ash that was pouring over the whole town. This downpour in November of 1985 marked the beginning of the eruption of Nevado del Ruiz, a long-dormant volcano in the Cordillera Central. Nobody would have imagined that in the next few frightening hours, Armero would become a grave for nearly all its citizens.

The roar of destruction echoed through the town and brought with it a formidable torrent of molten mud and rocks. The eruption of the Arenas crater inside the 18,000-foot peak melted the mountain's icecap, sending devastating floods and mud slides rushing down into the Chinchina and Lagunilla river valleys.

The eruption of Nevado del Ruiz killed 22,800 people and destroyed 50,000 acres of farmland, 20,000 heads of cattle and 5,000 buildings. The town of Armero was virtually buried under the mud and several smaller local towns were nearly destroyed. The enormity of the devastation made the grim task of searching for survivors practically impossible. Those who had fled to the hillsides awaited evacuation by helicopter clad in underwear or nightclothes encrusted with mud and covered with blood.

What made the disaster all the more pitiable is that five weeks before the eruption, American and Italian volcanologists had warned Colombian authorities that Nevado del Ruiz, dormant since 1845, was due to come to life soon. Minor eruptions had begun two months before the catastrophe, and government officials had begun evacuation planning and the plotting of likely paths of mud slides. The unavoidable, however, would not wait.

CITIES

The largest cities are Bogotá, with a population of five million people; Medellín and Cali, with two million each; and Barranquilla, with one million. Other large cities are Cartagena, Bucaramanga, Cúcuta, Manizales, Pereira, Santa Marta and Ibague. Many Colombian cities have grown rapidly in recent years due to immigration from rural areas, bringing the city population to two-thirds of the country's total population. The number of large cities in Colombia is uncharacteristic of Latin America, where the capital and two or three other cities account for most of the urbanization; perhaps it is because most of the land is uninhabitable.

BOGOTA

The full name of Colombia's capital is Santa Fe de Bogotá, after its original Indian name, Bacatá, meaning "beyond the cultivated lands." It is a sprawling metropolis like any other city. Situated in a high valley called the Sabana de Bogotá, it is more than 8,500 feet above sea level.

Bogotá is an artistic, cultural and intellectual capital, as well as the political center of Colombia. It is also becoming a major industrial center. As one of the oldest cities of the Western Hemisphere, it is the site of many stately colonial churches, homes and universities. Bogotá is really two cities—Bogotá Viejo (the old city) and Bogotá Nuevo (the new city).

Scenic narrow streets in the old quarter are lined with balconied buildings, spreading out from Plaza Bolívar, which is the heart of Bogotá Viejo. This is where the first inhabitants lived. Many of Bogotá's breathtaking churches date back to colonial times.

Bogotá has many museums tracing various aspects of Colombian art and history. The Colonial Museum has paintings of the Spanish colonial period; handicrafts are exhibited at the Museum of Popular Arts and Traditions. Works done by the Indians of San Agustín are displayed at the National Museum; the Museo del Oro contains more than 25,000 gold objects, the world's largest collection of pre-Columbian goldsmiths' work.

Bogotá, the capital, is the focal point of all political, economic and cultural activity in the country.

Middle-class inhabitants live in ultra-modern buildings in the northern part of the city, which also has embassies, large private residences and exclusive boutiques. The broad boulevards, modern skyscrapers and shopping centers of Bogotá Nuevo create a stark contrast to the quaint architecture of Bogotá Viejo. Working-class neighborhoods are in the southern and western areas of the city, where industrial plants are also found.

As in other Colombian cities, streets in Bogotá run in straight lines and are called *carreras* when running north to south, and *calles* when running east to west.

The immigration of people from the countryside has created crowded *turgurios*, or slums, with temporary housing and climbing unemployment, poverty and crime rates. Other problems common to major cities, such as heavy traffic and pollution, exist in Bogotá as well.

MEDELLIN

Colombia's second largest city is Medellín, known for its textile industry. In recent years, it has attained world visibility for being home of one of the largest cocaine-selling groups. Just outside Medellín is El Ranchito, one of the world's outstanding collections of orchids.

Medellín was settled in the late 1600s by Spaniards who came to mine the gold deposits, and today many natives are their descendants. As the mines gave out, early inhabitants quickly became proficient farmers and the region is currently the leading coffee-growing area in the country.

Medellín has overcome the handicaps of physical isolation and rugged terrain to develop into a flourishing city.

Called the "City of Eternal Spring," it has an agreeable climate and a dramatic mountain vista. There is an attitude of progress about the city, which boasts many modern hotels, banks, offices, shops and skyscrapers. Its flower-lined avenues are a pleasant surprise to visitors expecting to see the smoke stacks of an industrial city.

This bustling community is host to many flower festivals and exhibitions, and bullfights are of great enjoyment to the citizenry. On weekends during bullfighting season, La Marcarena, a 10,000-seat bullring, is the center of much enthusiasm.

CALI

Founded in 1536, Cali too is one of Colombia's old cities, but it has experienced exceptional growth over the last couple of decades. Many signs of colonial styles are still apparent in the city, however.

Cali is a manufacturing and distribution center which lies on the edge of Cauca, the country's vital agricultural valley. The valley is responsible

Below top: **The Plaza de Caicedo Cathedral is a striking example of Cali's colonial architecture.**

Below bottom: **Cartagena, the fortress city on the Caribbean coast. The ancient and the new harbor face each other.**

for 20% of Colombia's industrial output, composed mostly of paper and sugar production. Its altitude of 3,300 feet gives it a very pleasant climate all year, with significant rainfall during its two rainy seasons. Flooding can become a problem in lower sections of the city, and several earthquakes have hit Cali in the past few years.

In spite of its commercial focus, cultural and sporting endeavors are still enthusiastically pursued. Many sporting contests and art exhibitions are held in the city.

Some of Colombia's most hopeless slums have been in Cali, and in the past, filth, disease and poverty caused more than half the children to die before reaching five years of age.

CARTAGENA

One of the most picturesque towns in South America, Cartagena has some of the finest examples of 16th century architecture in the Western Hemisphere. In its early days, Cartagena was the most important fortified city of the Spanish Empire, and much of the fortification remains today. Sixteen miles of protective wall surround narrow streets and adobe buildings, providing an exceptional view. On one side is the Caribbean and on the other is the charming old section of the city.

The contrast between old and new is prominent. Houses in the new part of Cartagena are of varied styles. Many are brightly colored two-story homes with attractive gardens, patios and balconies. Within the old section of Cartagena remain seven fortresses that previously protected the harbor and the city. Street vendors and women carrying trays on their heads preserve the flavor of this picturesque place.

HISTORY

ALFONSO DE OJEDA in 1500 was the first Spaniard to reach the shores of what is now known as Colombia. At that time, it was inhabited by as many as eight different Indian groups, all of which spoke a different language. The population at that time was possibly as large as 700,000. The most advanced were the Chibchas, or Muisca as they called themselves. They largely lived as hunters and fishermen, but many lived by working the land and trading, and a good number were goldsmiths.

The coastal Indians proved so hostile that the earliest explorers withdrew quickly. But, the exquisite gold ornaments fashioned by the Indians provided such a lure that Spanish explorers spread the word of a land of fabulous treasure—they called it "El Dorado"—and set off for the Americas with the goal of bringing the treasure back to Spain.

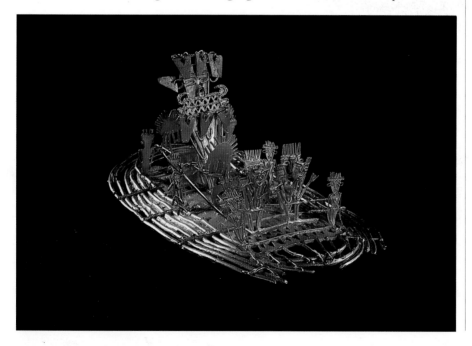

Left: **A replica of the Chibcha "El Dorado" raft is on display in Bogotá's Gold Museum.**

Opposite: **The mysterious ancient stone statues at San Agustín bear witness to Colombia's rich Indian heritage.**

THE LEGEND OF EL DORADO

The Chibchas, or Muiscas, believe that a meteor fell to the Earth and formed a great crater filled with water. In this lake, which is now called Guatavita, initiation rites for Chibcha chieftains were held. The chieftain's body was rubbed with a glue-like substance and he was then covered with gold dust. The golden leader was then rowed to the middle of the lake aboard a raft holding gifts to the gods. On the shore, tribesmen knelt in awe among blazing bonfires. The new chief would then dive into the water and wash the gold dust into the lake as an offering to the deities. The treasures from the raft were added to the lake and the people on the shores added precious items of their own.

This simple Chibcha ceremony was the basis for the legend of El Dorado, a term that now refers to any place where there is enormous wealth. The story inspired the Spanish to launch numerous explorations in search of the riches. The eventual conquest of the Chibcha ushered in the historical era of Colombia.

Courtesy of New York Public Library

SPANISH SETTLEMENTS

The first permanent Spanish settlements were made at Santa Marta in 1525 and at Cartagena in 1533. However, the interior of the country was not penetrated until 1536, when Gonzalo Jiménez de Quesada traveled up the Magdalena River. He and his men defeated the Chibcha Indians they encountered in the various mountain valleys and founded the city of Bogotá in 1538.

At about the same time, an expedition from neighboring Ecuador under the command of Sebastian de Belalcázar had come up the Cauca valley, and founded Pasto, Popayán and Cali in 1536. Another expedition led by Nicolaus de Federmann met up with Belalcázar's group as they both reached Bogotá, beginning a period of conflict among the various conquering groups.

Rather than fight, however, the three *conquistadors* submitted their cases to the court of Spain. Federmann received nothing. Belalcázar was named governor of Popayán, and Jiménez de Quesada was given the military title of marshal and was allowed to remain on the land he had won for Spain. He named the newly conquered land Nueva Granada and its capital Santa Fe de Bogotá.

In the 15th and 16th centuries, Spain grew into a naval power and colonized a big portion of South America.

Cartagena was fortified to defend the country from attacks by English and Dutch pirates who coveted the gold being shipped to Spain.

NUEVA GRANADA

In 1550, a royal government was established for the administration of Colombia. In that same year, gold was discovered in Antioquia. As soon as gold shipments to Spain commenced, English and Dutch pirates began their attacks on Spanish shipping and Caribbean ports. Fortunately, the interior of the country was able to develop undisturbed.

Despite Nueva Granada's great wealth, Spain was only mildly interested in this territory. For the first 200 years of Spanish rule, the land was governed by a president appointed by the viceroy of Peru.

During this time, however, Cartagena developed as the major port through which all trade with South America was supposed to travel. With the addition of the territory of present-day Ecuador and Venezuela, Colombia became a viceroyalty in its own right in 1739.

The Monument to Independence stands on the site where Bolívar and other patriots won their battle against the colonizers.

INDEPENDENCE

The movement for independence started in the 1790s after the French Revolution. Venezuelans revolted in 1796 and 1806, and an attempt to set up an independent government in Bogotá failed.

In May 1810, Cartagena declared independence. Bogotá followed one month later and six years of independence ensued. Spain regained the territory in 1816. Independence finally came in August 1819, when Simon Bolívar and his generals defeated the Spaniards at the Battle of Boyacá.

Though allies in the quest for independence, Bolívar and his generals could not agree on the new form of government. Bolívar preferred a strong central government, while José Antonio Páez and Francisco de Paula Santander pushed for a federation of sovereign states.

In 1821, the Constitution of Cúcuta formally set up the federation called the Republic of Colombia, which included Panama, Venezuela and Ecuador. Present-day Colombia was known as Nueva Granada. It was only in 1863 that it took the name of Colombia. Historians refer to the former federation as Gran Colombia to avoid confusion.

Bolívar was elected president of Gran Colombia while continuing the fight for Ecuador's liberation and the independence of Peru. In his absence, Santander, his vice president, governed the nation.

DICTATORSHIPS AND DEMOCRACY

The federation was doomed from the start. In 1827, Bolívar established a dictatorship, but had to resign in March 1839 because of opposition. Two years later, Santander became president and instituted a democratic state.

By 1849, two political parties were firmly established: the Conservatives, in favor of central government and closely tied with the Catholic Church, and the Liberals, favoring a federation of states and separation of church

Simon Bolívar, *El Libertador*, led the revolution which overthrew Spanish rule. His memory is worshiped throughout South America.

and state. From 1840 to 1880, the two parties alternated in power, amid much civil strife. But the economy and population grew, trade and communications improved, and Colombia was in an enviable position.

Poet Raphael Nuñez was elected president in 1880. Though a declared Liberal, he held conservative views. Nuñez ruled like a dictator until his death in 1896. He made Catholicism the state religion and restored a centralized government.

Meanwhile, the economy experienced little growth, and soon the War of a Thousand Days broke out. More than 100,000 people were killed, and the country was on the brink of economic collapse. Shortly after the restoration of peace, Panama seceded with the help of the United States. This interference caused bitter Colombian-American relations for many years.

The period between 1903 and 1930 was unusually stable. Colombia entered foreign trade vigorously, through coffee exportation. Multinational corporations invested in banana and petroleum production, and Colombia experienced some boom years in the 1920s. Railroads and power plants were built; but the affluence led to over-expansion and inflation.

"La Violencia" from 1948 to 1958 is one of the bloodiest periods in Colombian history.

LA VIOLENCIA

The Great Depression brought financial disaster. In 1930, the government started economic and social reforms. And in 1944, a new labor code provided for minimum wages, employee benefits and trade unions.

After the Second World War, there were severe political crises. Violence reached fever pitch with the assassination of popular leader Jorge Eliecer Gaitan in 1948. Thus began "La Violencia." Bogotá was rendered a shambles, and in the next 10 years, 200,000 persons lost their lives.

In 1958, a public agreement was reached. Under the accord, known as the National Front, the Conservative and Liberal parties agreed to rotate the presidency for 16 years. Each four-year administration ruled over a coalition government.

In recent years, Colombia has experienced the emergence of armed guerillas. At the end of 1985, they united to form one sizable faction which is represented in the congress. This is a positive sign that encourages the Colombians to deal with their social problems.

GOVERNMENT

COLOMBIA IS a democratic republic with a centralized government and separate executive, legislative and judicial branches. It is a basic structure of national government which is quite similar to that of the United States. It has a long history of democracy, which is quite notable in a continent known for its dictatorships.

The president is elected by direct vote for a four-year term and cannot serve more than one term in succession. As chief legislative executive, he has the power to approve or veto legislation. He appoints a cabinet of 13 ministers and is assisted in decision-making by a consulting body composed of 10 members called the Council of State. The president acts as commander-in-chief and directs internal affairs.

THE NATIONAL CONGRESS

The legislative branch is known as the National Congress. It is a bicameral (two-house) congress composed of a Chamber of Representatives and a Senate. Representatives and senators are elected and serve four-year terms. Each department is represented by two senators at large and an additional senator for every 200,000 people. There are two representatives for each department plus an additional one for every 100,000 people. Currently, there are 114 senators; representatives number 199.

Opposite: **On the walls of Bogotá, political posters jostle with bullfight notices for attention. Here gamins (street children) warm themselves at a fire lit with torn posters.**

PREAMBLE TO THE CONSTITUTION OF 1886

In the name of God, supreme source of all authority, and for the purpose of strengthening national unity and securing the benefits of justice, liberty and peace, we have decided to decree, and we do hereby decree, the following POLITICAL CONSTITUTION OF COLOMBIA.

Colombia is a democratic country where the government is voted in by the people. The seat of government is in the Congress Building in Bogotá.

THE JUDICIARY

The basic law of Colombia is the constitution of 1886. The system of courts includes a Supreme Court of Justice which tries cases involving interpretation of the constitution and impeachment. It also serves as the final court of appeal. Justices of this court are nominated by the president and elected by the congress. They face re-appointment every five years.

Administratively, Colombia is divided into 23 departments, or states, four territorial districts (*intendencias*), five special districts (*comisarias*), and the special district of Bogotá. Governors appointed by the president head each department and are also included in the executive branch.

At the local level, mayors of cities are elected by popular vote. Deputies for assemblies of the various department (state) and municipal councils are also chosen by direct vote.

VOTING AND ELECTIONS

Voting is open to all citizens who are over the age of 21. In August 1954, a special act was passed to allow women to take part in national elections. Colombians must register to vote and have a citizenship card. Voting is considered a legal right but not a duty, and there are no literacy or land ownership requirements. People not allowed to vote include members of the national police, active members of the armed forces and people who have lost their political rights by law.

Voter registration takes place at the municipal level, which means that there are local offices that handle the process. Although the requirements for voting are not strict, registration is somewhat complicated, and re-registering after moving to another district is very involved.

Polling places are supervised by a committee made up of two members of each political party. Committees report the results to the municipal registrar and the results are forwarded to the national registrar's office.

Colombia's political scene is dominated by two parties, the Liberals and the Conservatives. Elections are always strongly contested.

ECONOMY

THE DEVELOPMENT of the Colombian economy can be divided into four periods. The first ended in 1880, before which time the country had no stable exports to help buy goods that Colombia did not produce.

Coffee paved the way for the second period, which lasted until 1930. Exportation of this plentiful commodity paid for manufactured goods from abroad. Also during this time, industry developed near Medellín.

The third period saw industrialization on a national scale, beginning during the Great Depression. Through 1967, the economic policy of the country stressed industrialization. Revenue from coffee was used to purchase intermediate goods, or material for the factories that were being developed.

During the fourth period, the government encouraged the exportation of lesser goods to supplement coffee and refined petroleum. These supplementary exports were a reliable source of foreign currency.

Left: **Agriculture has always played an important role in the Colombian economy. Here, cotton is being harvested at Palmira.**

Opposite: **At a sugar mill in Santander, the sugarcane juice is reduced to brown sugar by boiling.**

PRIVATE ENTERPRISE

Private enterprise is stronger in Colombia than in most Latin American countries. In fact, one of the most dynamic capitalist projects in Latin America took place around Medellín at the beginning of this century. The success of that venture convinced everyone that the government could not guide the economy as effectively as the private sector.

The government, however, does get involved in the economy in unique ways. The Colombian economy is defined as a mixed economy: there are separate functions for the government, for private Colombian businesses and for foreign multinational corporations. The government's role is considered essential to leading the nation to complete development. The government owns transportation systems, roads and telecommunications, and it produces the country's electricity. Also, as owner of the subsoil, the administration is expected to develop energy resources. The state is also directly involved in the economy through its control of tariffs, taxation and exchange rates.

An interesting aspect of the way the private sector operates is that it does not invest in an enterprise considered to be essential to national development. However, when the industries become profitable, the government sells them to private corporations.

Colombia's major trading partners are the United States, Germany, Japan, Venezuela, the Netherlands and Brazil.

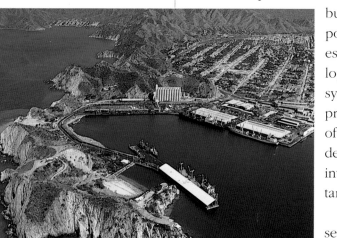

Santa Marta, on the Caribbean coast, has become a popular tourist resort in recent years.

AGRICULTURE

Colombia is primarily an agricultural nation, largely dependent on coffee. Fifteen years ago, about half of the population was involved in agriculture; today, less than one-third of the work force is engaged in it. One quarter of the nation's land is used for agriculture; about 10% of that is devoted to crop production and the rest utilized for livestock pasture.

Colombia produces a wide range of crops, from bananas that need warm temperatures to potatoes which flourish in cooler temperatures. However, many people have to farm on inclines that erode easily, and deforestation of the Andean region is intensifying the erosion problem. Many farms in the highlands are quite small, and the owners rely on simple methods. Their primitive ways limit them to subsistence farming, which means that their work provides all the goods needed by the family, with no significant surplus for sale.

COFFEE Though coffee remains the nation's chief agricultural product, it makes up only about 4% of the gross domestic product. Colombia is the second largest producer of coffee in the world. Because the beans grow best between 4,300 and 6,600 feet, the greatest concentration of coffee farms is near Medellín. Coffee is a labor intensive crop and the farms are typically small.

Colombia is the second largest producer of coffee in the world. Hand-picking and the fact that the bushes are grown in the shade account for its high quality.

33

BANANAS Bananas, another significant export, are grown along the Caribbean coast. Foreign multinational corporations were initially involved in banana production; however, private Colombian organizations have entered the market also. As much as 40% of the total banana production is consumed in Colombia, and this crop is thought to bring the farmer the best income return per acre.

Another contribution to the Colombian economy is the export of fresh cut flowers which earns a substantial income.

SUGARCANE Sugarcane, much of which is made into unrefined brown sugar, or *panela*, is planted throughout the hot areas of the nation, especially in the Cauca river valley and on the central Pacific coast. In contrast to a well-defined sugarcane-growing season in many other places throughout the world, Colombia's sugarcane harvest continues almost year round because of the climate in the growing regions. The warm days and steady rainfall throughout the year provide permanent employment for cane-cutters.

FLOWERS Fresh cut flowers are another important commodity. This commercial activity is concentrated in the *sabana*, or treeless plain near Bogotá, and provides employment for about 15,000 people. Colombian flower producers provide carnations, orchids and other popular flowers for the export market.

Cattle is being herded by the *vaqueros* in the eastern *llanos*, one of the most important cattle raising regions.

CATTLE Livestock raising is carried out in scattered areas throughout the country, though major concentrations are in the Sabana de Bogotá and in the eastern plains. Beef is the dominant meat produced in the country, and in the early 1980s the cattle population was estimated at more than 26 million, which means that there were almost as many cows as people. Recently, however, cattle ranchers have met with a number of problems that have made it difficult for them to increase their beef production. Nutritional deficiencies among the cattle are the most troubling of these problems.

FISHING The fishing industry is developing along both coasts of the country and in the Magdalena river valley. There is an abundance of fish in the coastal waters and the many rivers. About 19 varieties of freshwater fish are caught by fishermen, but two types of catfish account for the majority of the recorded yearly catch. Buenaventura and Tumaco are the main fishing ports.

The subsoil of Colombia is extremely rich in minerals, and it was mainly the abundance of gold that led to the Spanish colonization.

MINING

Colombia is extremely rich in minerals, having mined gold and emeralds since pre-colonial days. During the colonial period, it was the largest contributor of gold to the Spanish coffers, and it continues to be the world's leading producer of emeralds, accounting for 95% of all emerald production. Colombia is also the largest of South America's producers of gold and the only South American country to produce platinum.

Today's wealth of minerals includes not only gold, platinum and emeralds, but also nickel, lead, mercury, manganese, coal and salt.

The Guajira peninsula has a valuable deposit of clean-burning coal that is easily mined by open-pit or strip mining techniques because it is near the surface. The Colombian government and several industrial firms have spent millions to develop this mine, which may contain as much as 60% of South America's coal reserves.

ENERGY PRODUCTION

The oil wells in the Magdalena river valley have been supplying most of the nation's crude oil since the 1920s. Additional oil deposits have been found in numerous areas, including the basin of the Catatumbo River, in the central Caribbean and Pacific areas and in the eastern *llanos*. These finds have led geologists to think that there is more oil near the Andes. In the mid-1970s, Colombia began importing oil to augment its production. But the nation has now regained its self-sufficiency, and has even become a modest exporter of oil.

This oil refinery at Barrancabermeja is run by the state which is responsible for developing the energy resources of the country.

To keep up with its energy demands, Colombia makes use of its waterways. The abundance of rivers, coupled with the high rainfall, have led experts to say that Colombia has one of the greatest hydroelectric potentials in the world. Hydroelectricity facilities are in the Bogotá-Cali-Medellín area, which is known as the "industrial triangle."

The Cauca Valley Authority is headquartered in Cali. This corporation's focus is flood control, improved farming techniques through irrigation and development of electrical power. This successful venture tripled Cali's electrical power in its first eight years. Currently, up to 70% of existing power systems use hydroelectricity, and the figure is estimated to rise to 90% in the near future.

TRANSPORTATION

Topography is a contributing factor to obstacles in transportation. The terrain of the Andes and landslides due to heavy rainfall in the heavily populated highlands make road and rail travel difficult and expensive to develop. In some areas, mules are sometimes the only means of transporting people and material across the terrain; in more developed spots, aerial cable cars are the only option.

RIVER NAVIGATION River travel is also very important. In fact, before the railroad from Bogotá to Santa Marta was built, the Magdalena River was the major travel route between the Caribbean coast and the interior. Not too long ago, almost 95% of all commercial inland water transport was carried out on the Magdalena. In times of drought, however, this type of travel becomes impossible.

ROADS The country has nearly 68,000 miles of roads, but only 6,500 miles are paved. The irregular terrain makes the construction of roads a very costly venture. There are, however, three important road systems which run north to south between the mountain systems. In addition, the 2,300-mile-long Simon Bolívar Highway runs from Guayaquil in Ecuador east through Colombia to Caracas in Venezuela, and a section of the Pan-American Highway connects Bogotá, Cali and Venezuela.

RAIL The National Railway System network, which is 2,100 miles long, is nearly totally government-owned, and it is currently being expanded. Great railway expansion took place in the 1940s and 1950s, when the network finally connected the highlands with both coasts. The Atlantic rail line was opened in 1961 and runs from Bogotá to Santa Marta. Buenaventura and Bogotá are connected by the Pacific rail line. Freight and passenger railway traffic reached its height in the 1960s, when truck and airline services surpassed rail traffic popularity.

Much cargo that would have moved by land in other countries moves by air in Colombia, mainly by AVIANCA (Aerovias Nacionales de Colombia).

AVIATION To surmount the difficulties that its mountain systems present to cross-country travel, Colombia became a trailblazer in the field of domestic civil aviation. In 1919, Colombia founded its own airline, AVIANCA, which is now the nation's major international airline. This thriving service now flies direct to numerous cities in the United States, Canada and Europe. El Dorado, Colombia's international airport, is located in Bogotá.

A special technique for washing and drying coffee has enabled the Colombian "milds" to fetch high prices on the world market. It is still a major export.

FOREIGN TRADE

Colombia's imports are mainly raw materials and intermediate goods. Its major exports, as mentioned previously, are coffee, coal and fuel oil.

The United States and Colombia have long been chief trading partners. Prior to 1950 more than 70% of Colombia's exports went to the United States, and more than 60% of Colombia's import activities involved American goods. Since that time, new markets have been opened in Europe, and Colombia has played a key role in the Andean Common Market. This group's major goal is to increase trade among its member nations. Evidence of its success is that neighboring countries are significant trading partners with Colombia.

AN UNUSUAL EXPORT

A rather unlikely Colombian commodity that is of great interest to the scientific community is the kokoa frog. For the last couple of decades, American scientists have been hiring boys from a village on the Pacific coast called Playa de Oro to catch these amazing amphibians, for their toxins are being studied for possible use as anesthetics and heart medicine.

Chocó Indians have been tipping their darts with the poison from these yellow-striped frogs for quite some time now. In the early 1820s, a British Navy captain described during his explorations how Chocó hunters prepared their darts with poison by causing the frogs to sweat. The Indians dipped the dart in the white foam perspiration. One tiny frog, which is small enough to fit in a teaspoon, produced enough poison for 50 arrows.

Some 150 years later, Indian boys capture the frogs in little cages made of banana leaves and bring their booty to the American scientists' camp. There, the scientists remove the skins of the frogs and soak them in alcohol. The resultant liquid is bottled and shipped to the laboratories in the United States for research.

COLOMBIANS

COLOMBIA'S ETHNIC MAKEUP is as diverse as its topography. Its population descends mainly from three racial groups—Amerindian, African strains and European, or Spanish. Armed with a knowledge that objective racial classification is impossible, the national census ceased reporting population figures by race in 1919. Thus, with no official figures available, a mid-1989 estimate of the 31,200,000 people provides the following breakdown: 58% *mestizo* (Indian-Spanish), 20% white, 14% mulatto, 7% black/black-Indian and 1% Indian.

Though racial characteristics are important to the people of Colombia, they do not carry the same significance as in the United States. Nonetheless, many Colombians continue to identify themselves according to ancestry and socio-cultural status. And the varying groups can still be found in concentrations that reflect patterns set up by the colonial social system.

Unlike the other nations to the south, Colombia is a predominantly white and *mestizo* country. These two Guajiro girls (opposite) and this man from the Cauca valley (above) are *mestizos*.

For example, Indian tribes that survived the Spanish Conquest are found in scattered clusters, isolated from other ethnic groups, in areas not penetrated by others, such as the Guajira peninsula. *Mestizos*, who had been peasants in earlier times, live mostly in the highlands, where Spanish conquerors mingled with native women. In recent years, however, many *mestizos* have migrated to the cities and have become members of the urban working class. Blacks and mulattos who are not following the trend of moving to the cities continue to live mainly along the coasts and in the lowlands of the *cordilleras* where there are few Indians. Whites predominantly live in the cities.

NATIVE TRIBES

A variety of Indian cultures flourished in Colombia before the 16th century and the arrival of the Europeans. The Quimbayas were the people of the western slopes of the Cordillera Central. Skilled craftsmen of this tribe made elaborate jewelry: necklaces, rings, breastplates and nose ornaments. To fashion these items, they poured molten gold into wax molds that they had developed. Their ornaments followed a natural theme: the gilded objects were molded after eagles, owls, birds and the like. They also did considerable work with clay.

The Chibchas comprised almost one-third of the pre-Columbian population. This tribe called itself Muisca, but the Spaniards referred to it as the Chibcha, which meant "people" in the Muisca language. They lived mainly in the Cundinamarca Basin, which is where Bogotá is today.

The Chibchas were a very civilized people. This deeply religious group lived in villages and organized itself along class lines; a person's rank and status were inherited from the mother. To show one's position within the society, both men and women often painted their bodies with various designs.

The Chibchas had an efficient system of communal land laws. None of their land was privately owned, and the tribe was subdivided into groups that occupied distinct provinces. Each territory was ruled by a local chief who reported to a more powerful *cacique*, or chieftain. *Caciques* reported to one of the two supreme leaders.

The Chibcha civilization was very skilled in farming, mining and metalcraft. These Indians grew mainly corn, beans and potatoes. They also mined salt, which they traded for other minerals. Though the Chibchas considered salt to be most valuable, they had an immense fortune in emeralds and gold. Many of the valuables were buried with the dead, but

The Indian tribes west of the Magdalena River were virtually wiped out by the Spaniards. Those tribes which have survived to this day are usually small and mostly keep to themselves.

Weaving is a traditional craft of native Indians. Here a Cofan woman makes a *mochila* (bag).

fortunately, others have survived to the present time and can be seen in Bogotá's Museo del Oro.

The Indian culture in modern Colombia evolved from the Quimbaya, Chibcha and Carib tribes. There are still a good number of Indian tribes, many living in the eastern two-thirds of the country. Some remain isolated, such as the Motilón, who resist all contact with outsiders. This tribe has been known in fairly recent times to perch in mountain retreats and attack missionary groups or oil company employees with poisoned arrows and blow guns.

Another Indian tribe in Colombia today is the Yagua Indians of the Amazon jungle. The Yagua Indians live in huts on stilts that protect them from floods caused by torrential rains. The men are hunters and fishermen. There are approximately 3,000 Yagua Indians.

In tribes such as the Chimilas and the Sanha of the Sierra Nevada de Santa Marta mountain region, men and boys live in a temple where they spin cotton and weave cloth while women and girls live in houses with thatched roofs.

Despite the rigid social structure, the various races live together in harmony. Urban Indians have adapted to the general way of life.

SOCIAL SYSTEM

The structure of Colombian society is based on 16th century colonial Spanish traditions. At that time, black slaves from Africa were introduced to the coastal regions, and the practice continued throughout the next 300 years. Some slaves were taken to the plantation and mining regions, and others escaped to the interior. Most, however, remained in slavery until its abolition in the mid-1800s.

The Spanish devised a hierarchical society in which they became the prestigious, wealthy and powerful. The lower echelons were filled by the slaves and indigenous tribes. The pattern of settlement left frontier areas and less inhabitable lands to the less fortunate—the non-whites.

Colombian society is still distinguished by its pronounced status differences and limited upward social mobility. The class system is more flexible in cities than in rural areas. In rural society there is a rigid structure with virtually no possibility of upward movement. The extreme class differences are often troubling to foreigners, but Colombians accept these social conditions as a natural part of their lives.

Four layers comprise the Colombian social system: the upper, middle and lower classes, and the masses. The three classes are distinguished by the level of participation in and understanding of the national society, whereas the masses are known for the abject poverty and illiteracy that keep them powerless.

Other factors that differentiate the classes are wealth, lifestyle, family background, education and occupation. Education is generally considered to be the key to vertical social mobility.

WHITES Because of the social ranking set up during colonial times, white skin became associated with being Spanish and was, therefore, of high status. Whites continue to hold the highest positions in the government, economy and society. Though whites are and always have been a minority of the total population, being a part of that group implied a following of the European behavioral patterns and teachings of the Catholic Church, and this supremacy influenced the rest of society.

Whites still emphasize colonial ideas such as the superiority of mental pursuits, and they encourage genteel and creative activities and professions for those with financial security. Careers in business and industry are considered very acceptable for those who are not from the most wealthy and prestigious families. The importance of racial purity varies from region to region and may not matter as much as an old and respected Spanish surname.

The *mestizos* identify with the whites and have adopted western styles of dressing.

47

MESTIZOS Racial mixing has occurred in Colombia from the earliest years, and Colombians often refer to themselves as a *mestizo* or mixed nation. Approximately 60% of the population is of mixed origin, and these people are found in all social classes, occupations and regions. One of the most unifying factors within this group is the general perception that the status of *mestizo* or mulatto is better than that of Indian or black. Another interesting sociological factor is that *mestizos* are said to identify with the dominant white group. Similarly, the mulatto identifies with the black group, which may make upward social and economic mobility more difficult for them.

BLACKS Blacks continue to reflect distribution patterns of the colonial period, with the greatest number living in the lowland areas on the Pacific and Atlantic coasts and along the Cauca and Magdalena rivers. In Chocó blacks and mulattos represent 80% of the population.

The black groups in Chocó are quite distinctive in their music, marital practices and funeral rites. The distinctive music, more than any other element, makes Chocoan blacks aware of their identity. Many black Chocoan men are polygynous, which means that they are married to, or live with, more than one woman. Funeral rites in this region continue for nine days and include nightly prayers, heavy consumption of alcohol and participation in betting games. These distinctions are cultural remnants of their African and slave heritages. The activities reinforce a sense of identity among the blacks in the region.

Few blacks have become prominent on the national scene, and Colombians consider the living conditions of blacks in Buenaventura to be a national disgrace.

A SEPARATE PEOPLE

As the pilgrims crossed the Atlantic Ocean on the *Mayflower* to reach the New World, a sister ship, the *Seaflower*, headed for San Andrés Island. The English puritans settled on the island, but these early settlers were replaced by buccaneers who preyed upon Spanish ships, and eventually by the Spanish. After famous pirate Henry Morgan wrested the island from the Spanish, it remained largely uninhabited for more than 100 years. In fact, in 1780, a visitor from the United States reported that only 12 families were living on San Andrés.

In 1822, the islands of San Andrés and nearby Providencia came under Colombian rule. Since then, they have become steady coconut suppliers for the United States and a popular vacation spot for Colombians and many North Americans.

Though these glittering islands have belonged to Colombia for more than a century and a half, inhabitants have so maintained their isolation that they have not even adopted the Spanish language or taken up the national religion—Roman Catholicism. These islanders retain the Protestant religion, continue to speak English and regard themselves as a distinct group from the mainland Colombians.

COSTUME

City dwellers dress in the same styles as people in North American cities. Colombian youths are eager to follow fashion trends; *molas* (embroidered shirts) are worn with as much frequency as designer jeans and shirts.

Regional differences in attire are really dependent on climate. In hot areas on the Pacific coast, men seldom wear coats. There is also often a correlation between the size of the city and the elegance of dress. People in Bogotá have been referred to as *currutacos*, or dandies, in part because of their finery.

In the country, most articles are homemade. There are several basic rural garments: the *poncho, ruana,* and *bayetón.* Each one is a cloak with an opening in the middle for the head. It hangs from front to back, leaving the arms free. *Bayetones* are nearly ankle length; *ruanas,* the most common of the three, hang to a little below the waist; and *ponchos* fall between the other two lengths.

Among low income groups, *ruanas* are also used as blankets. Woolen *ruanas* are remarkably waterproof because natural oils are left in the material.

The *pañolón* is another traditional woman's garment which resembles the *ruana.* This shawl is customarily made of cotton or silk. Girls and younger women wear fringed *pañolones* of bright color, whereas elderly women are clad in black or darkly colored fabrics.

Indian women of tribes that have little contact with civilization are usually bare breasted. The children run freely without clothes.

Typical shoes are fiber slippers and sandals. Footwear is an indicator of status, and many rural people prefer to work barefoot. In some groups it is also regarded as ostentatious to wear shoes.

Above: **This Guambino family shows off the typical garments of Indians living in high altitude.**

Opposite: **Ruanas are worn by both men and women, and can double as blankets too.**

LIFESTYLE

IN COLOMBIA, lifestyle also varies according to region. In Leticia, Colombia's southernmost city, inhabitants depend on trapping and fishing for their livelihood. Even when meeting in the town square, residents must be wary of the hazards that one encounters in the heart of the jungle, for Leticia lies in the Amazon valley.

On the *llanos*, cowboys drive the herds all day in the areas where much of the country's meats and cereals are produced. *Vaqueros* (cowboys) wearing traditional straw hats can be seen tethering cattle and tending to livestock such as mules, pigs, goats, chickens and sheep.

Fishing villages and harbors teem along the Colombian coastline, and people rely on the ocean for their living. Men work on the docks shirtless, loading and unloading cargo with bandannas around their necks.

In the populated areas of the mountains, coffee plantations abound and are the main source of income. Residents of this area also fish in the clear mountain streams. A typical working day of coffee plantation workers begins around 8 a.m. with plastic buckets tied with string around their waist. As they fill the buckets, the beans are emptied into a plastic sack. Workers move very quickly because they are paid according to the amount they pick. An experienced coffee picker handles about 110 pounds of beans each day. After working continuously for four hours, the worker takes the sacks full of coffee beans to the plantation manager, who measures what has been picked, and the worker receives the wages for the day.

City workers are accountants, doctors, lawyers, office and cafeteria workers, janitors and the like.

Above: **In the streets of Colombian towns, like those of any other town in the world, one can see all sorts of people, from the well-dressed office worker to the street vendor.**

Opposite: **The stereotyped cowboy comes alive in the *llanos*, the cattle-breeding region.**

FAMILY LIFE

The family is a very important social unit in Colombia. When a Colombian refers to the family, he or she is speaking about a wide circle of kinship that consists of several generations. It is what a North American would probably think of as the extended family.

The function and structure of the family do vary, though, depending once again on regional and socio-economic factors. Typically, children live with their families until they marry, and often afterward. Young adults from upper-middle and upper-class families are starting to get their own apartments before marriage, but it is still quite common for newly married couples to live with their large families until they save enough to set out on their own.

The ideal of the family as a close-knit unit is still very much present in all social and racial groups.

Family ties are somewhat weaker in urban centers than in rural areas, but households are usually large regardless of locale. Grandparents and other aging relatives are customarily part of the household in addition to the core family unit of mother, father and children. Cousins and their relatives can also join the family circle for extended periods of time when necessary. The set-up is usually flexible; only the rural upper class has traditional patriarchal domiciles, in which married sons and their families remain in the home.

Sunday is family day. Colombians are likely to visit their families on this day, for the importance of kinship is greatly emphasized. It is the basis of much social and business interaction.

Family involvement is also a large part of the Colombian business world. There are a lot of family-run businesses in which few, if any, positions of importance are given to outsiders. The spirit of family loyalty permits employers to feel safe in hiring, for the boss believes that the relatives' true strengths and weaknesses are well known among the family; there are no surprises from the new employee. Likewise, the sense of family loyalty will induce the employee to keep the boss's best interests at heart.

Among lower socio-economic groups, the household membership and structure of the family can be considerably different from those of the middle and upper classes. The reason for this is that formal marriage may not be the foundation of the family relationship. Sometimes the father is not a permanent resident of the home, and the mother is the chief authority in the family. This is most prevalent in Chocó, where in the 1960s, about one-third of the households were headed by women.

The extended family ties are often weakened in the lower-class family by the ever-increasing need to migrate to urban centers to find employment. But in keeping with the Hispanic uniformity in family life, rural migrants will move to areas where other relatives have previously relocated, and the pattern of extended-family living is resumed.

Family background and name are most important to those higher up on the social ladder. Colombia's most respected families are descended from 16th century Spanish settlers. Families with this distinction proudly display crests above the doors of their homes. A sense of pride is kept alive by a tradition of telling stories of the lives and deeds of ancestors.

Extended families are a feature of Colombian life. In certain regions, households are headed by women since the men may not always be present in the home.

COMPADRAZGO

Kinship lines become stretched even further by a traditional Hispanic relationship known as *compadrazgo*. This is a spiritual relationship that has to do with Catholic baptismal godparenthood. In this relationship, social and emotional bonds are created when a godparent accepts serious responsibilities for a child, and in turn, gets great respect from the child. But it is more complex than this; a spiritual bond is also created between the parents and the godparents. While godchildren refer to their godfather as *padrino* and godmother as *madrina*, parents of the children acknowledge the importance of their bond with the godparents by calling them *compadre* and *comadre*. These terms denote both friendship and companionship.

Every Colombian has a set of godparents, sometimes several sets, who take a personal interest in his or her development through life.

Colombians may have several sets of godparents, chosen at various important milestones in their lives. But the *padrino* and *madrina de bautismo* (baptismal godparents) are by far the most important. These godparents often see to the religious education of the child, and it is not unusual for an orphaned godchild to be adopted by his or her baptismal godparents. It is a lifelong relationship of great love and respect.

The cherished godparental relationship is not limited to Colombians of Hispanic descent. Chibcha Indian godparents are involved in personal occasions such as the first cutting of fingernails, earlobe piercing and the first cutting of hair. The *padrinos de sutas*, or those who cut the child's hair, are said to be the most honored.

DATING AND MARRIAGE

Dating without chaperones has recently become more common, especially among educated families in cities. Young Colombians develop exclusive relationships rather quickly, and they regard North American young people as promiscuous because of their tendency to "play the field."

Most Colombians get married, with the exception of the people from areas where native and African heritage has a great influence. There it is more usual for trial marriage to be practiced. Some communities will openly acknowledge this as a legitimate pre-marriage stage.

Since 1973 civil marriage has been legal in Colombia. Prior to that, only Catholic marriages were valid for Catholics. Nonetheless, many people look down on civil ceremonies, as it is felt that there is less commitment to marriages of this type. Catholic marriage is viewed as an ideal and as the legal, social and sexual basis of the family.

Religious marriage also connotes social status, and many Colombians see marriage as a means of social mobility. Young women can marry a man of great status and wealth, and their parents are always hopeful that this will happen. But the upper class is reluctant to wed persons of a lower social status. Matchmaking is not uncommon among the aristocracy, with a second or third cousin often being the chosen match.

Young Colombians do not normally make friends with persons of the opposite sex. North American-style dating is still looked down upon.

ROLES OF MEN AND WOMEN

"Macho" is a well-known term in North America, but it is not clearly defined. *Machismo* (being macho) is actually a Hispanic concept that distinguishes masculine attributes. It is a guideline for the male image and does not have the negative connotations created in the United States.

For the Latin American man, the image is that of being strong, respected, protective, and capable of providing for his wife and family. Though aggressiveness is something that North Americans associate with being macho, aggressiveness of the Colombian man actually varies according to social class, with middle and upper-class men being less brutish than those of the lower classes.

Women aspire to a socially-approved image also, with much emphasis placed on being feminine. This desired image can be seen in the way Colombian women dress, and in their appearance in general. The women of Bogotá, *bogotanas*, dress fashionably even when running errands or just staying around the house. This feminine image is so prevalent that travel guide booklets list the beautiful women of Cali as one of the city's main attractions!

ROLES WITHIN THE FAMILY

Family roles are also clearly defined. Everyone knows his or her responsibilities and the expected behavior. The father heads the family and his authority is the last word. As the chief, he expects his wife to be respectful and aware of his desires before her own. Colombian fathers are protective of their wives and children, and are diligent about keeping them away from what they consider to be negative outside influences.

The Colombian woman is expected to be a good wife, mother and hostess. She is the manager of the household, keeps things running smoothly and entertains with style and grace. If she performs her wifely role adequately, she is even considered an asset to her husband's career. Colombian women generally feel that their first duty is to raise children, which includes providing them with social graces and moral instruction.

Until recently, women of the upper class had never been allowed to work outside the home; the only acceptable activity was charitable volunteer work. Even social activities were limited to home and the school, and parties were chaperoned. Now, many upper-class women are well educated and enjoy careers in a variety of fields. More legal rights have been granted to women, and their participation and involvement in public affairs, government, and higher education is ever-increasing.

More and more women are going out to work nowadays, some even taking up "men's" professions, like this young engineer who works at a refinery.

Limitations have always been fewer for the middle and lower-class women. It has generally been an economic requirement for these wives to be employed outside the home and contribute their paychecks to the family budget, or to work out in the fields alongside their husbands. Unfortunately, wages remain low for these women.

THE WORK WEEK

The only day of rest in Colombia is Sunday. There are 18 holidays, and only six are not religious. These are New Year's Day, Labor Day (May 1), Independence Day (July 20), Battle of Boyacá (August 7), Columbus Day (October 12) and Independence of Cartagena (November 11).

In the industrial centers, the day begins between 8 and 8:30 a.m. and ends between 6:30 and 7 p.m. On farms and in the torrid zone, laborers may begin their workday at 6 or 7 a.m. Government offices are open from 8 a.m. to noon and again from 2 p.m. to 6 p.m.

Most businesses close for an hour and a half at midday, and workers go home for lunch, except in the city, because of traffic congestion. On farms, workers' wives will usually bring lunch to the fields.

VISITING

Relatives are the most frequent visitors in the Colombian home. A new guest would be entertained in the living room.

Colombians are not inhospitable. Visiting is quite pleasant when an invitation is extended. But if no time or date is mentioned, it is not a true invitation. When the invitation is repeated, it is usually more specific and a real date and time are arranged.

Evenings start later than in the United States, perhaps even after 9 p.m. Supper time in Colombia is around 8 p.m., but when company comes, everyone dines at 10 or 11 p.m. Drinks and snacks are served earlier.

Colombians entertain formally. Dress clothing is worn and dinners consist of many courses. Though the hostess will offer several helpings, she will not expect the guests to overeat. Colombians leave a small amount of food on their plates to show that the food was plentiful.

Colombians work from Monday through Friday and half a day on Saturday. Labor laws prohibit anyone from working more than 48 hours a week.

MARKET DAYS

Though rural life is sometimes rugged and a lot of hard work, the people of the country do enjoy some recreation. One thing they especially look forward to is market days.

One day a week is designated as market day. People from miles around travel to the nearest village to enjoy the festivities. All modes of transportation are used, not only to bring the produce, animals and handicrafts to the market, but also to transport the many country dwellers. Open-air buses crammed with passengers are seen on the road next to *burros* and push carts.

The main square in the village is the location for the marketplace. Goods and wares are spread out on wooden stands or stacked on the ground. Chickens strut past as people bargain with their friends and neighbors.

Market days are a great opportunity for the country people to visit, tell stories and purchase a variety of goods.

The "classroom" for the Noanama children is just an open hut built on stilts in the rainforest.

EDUCATION

At least 10% of the national budget must be spent on education, but the government spends almost as much on education as on all other social services combined. Now, free education is available to all, although more well-to-do families prefer private education.

There is still a prejudice toward the superior status of private education. Public elementary schools are known as *escuelas* which simply means "schools." Private elementary and high schools are called *colegios*, which translates as "colleges." The practice of sending middle-class children to private schools is very common.

In spite of the increases in government spending on education, some problems remain in the public education system; in the countryside, for example, there are sometimes not enough seats available in the schools. Although all children between the ages of 5 and 16 must attend school, among the poorest families, education is not a priority. The income that the children can earn from work is needed to keep the family going.

ELEMENTARY   Free elementary education consists of two years of kindergarten and five years of elementary school. Entrance into high school is dependent on completion of the elementary program.

HIGH SCHOOL   High school programs take six years to complete. Students can then be admitted to an institute of higher education.

VOCATIONAL   The Colombian system is slowly adding a vocational focus to its high school level programs. This change is intended to prepare students to meet the country's need for skilled labor in both agriculture and industry. This new emphasis is a real change from previous patterns of education which concentrated on preparing high school students to enter colleges and universities.

COLLEGE   More than 270,000 students, some of whom are children of the working class, attend 50 universities in Colombia. There are perhaps another 60 additional institutions of higher education in the country.

Today there is more emphasis on vocational training, such as fashion design.

Because of the challenging terrain and overwhelming poverty, often there is no way for children to get to school, and education by radio and television has been very successful. Colombia was the first South American country to use radio for this purpose. Rural people would gather around a radio set up in a public place, and transmitted over the air waves were lessons in reading, writing, history and geography. Television was added to the rural educational system in the early 1980s in order to reach all areas of the country in a more contemporary and effective manner.

HOUSING

Housing is designed in many different styles and built from different types of material because of the varied climate and income levels within the country. Classic colonial mansions and modern ranch-style houses can be found in the cities and their suburbs, while on the outskirts stand the most desperate slums called *turgurios*, where unemployment, poverty and crime rates are all high.

In rural areas, a large ranch of an upper-class family may be located near the small landholding of a subsistence farmer. In remote areas, people live in bamboo or thatched *tambos*, which are built on stilts that hold the structure about six feet above the land or water. In swampy areas, they keep the water from getting into the houses, and in dry regions, they protect the residents from snakes, dangerous insects and other wildlife that might cause harm. To enter, countryfolk climb up a notched stilt. Other rural homes are very simple; often there is no electricity or running water.

Until recently, rural housing had been generally inferior to urban housing, but heavy urban migration by persons desperate to make a living and support a family has caused the cities to struggle to keep up with the demand for new housing. Medellín's effort to keep up with housing needs is further complicated by its position. It faces mountain barriers in nearly every direction; it has no means of spreading out. The housing trend in Medellín and other large cities is toward tall, modern apartment buildings.

In Leticia at the edge of the Amazon forest, houses are built on stilts for safety purposes.

In La Candelaria, Bogotá's old section, houses form a solid wall facing the street.

AT HOME IN BOGOTA

Houses in Bogotá form a solid wall facing the sidewalk. There are no side yards and neighbors cannot visit with one another over a fence because the rear patio is surrounded by a high wall. There are also no back doors.

The *bogotano* home has two floors and no basement. The first floor windows are covered by iron bars or ornamental grillwork for security. Most homes also have maid's quarters, giving direct access to the kitchen, garage and service patio. This is where the maid washes the clothes. She also receives goods delivered through the garage.

Most modern homes have a patio in the rear of the house. Part of it is a garden, usually accessible from the living or dining room.

The maid is responsible for the first-floor chores, including cooking, washing, ironing and delivery acceptance. The señora tends to the chores upstairs, where the bedrooms and bathrooms are located.

A lot of time is spent upstairs. The señora stays in the bedroom and even entertains her women friends there. The living room is seldom used, and the family congregates in the upstairs hallway.

65

RELIGION

THE COLOMBIAN CONSTITUTION guarantees freedom of worship, but nearly all Colombians are Catholic. The Catholic Church in Colombia is known as one of the most conservative and traditional in Latin America. The parish church is considered the heart of most communities.

Catholicism has been the established religion since the 1500s. There has long been a great emphasis on the formal aspects of Catholicism, and most Colombians regularly observe holy days, attend Mass and receive the sacrament. In fact, attendance at Mass among both men and women is one of the highest in Latin America.

The constitution of 1886 gave special status to the Church and the concordat of 1887 made specifications about the Colombian government. (A concordat is an agreement between a pope and a government for the

Left: **Jesus' triumphant entry into Jerusalem is marked by a procession held on Palm Sunday one week before Easter.**

Opposite: **The San Pedro Claver Church in Cartagena. Catholicism is the major religion of Colombia, and the church is the common feature of all areas of settlement.**

The Holy Week procession is an important part of the rituals of the Catholic Church.

regulation of church matters.) However, in 1853 Colombia was the first Latin American country to pass a law that separated Church and State. Both the concordat and constitution remained in effect until 1973, when a new concordat was issued. Under the new agreement, the Church lost its stronghold on education, the territories occupied by Indians and regulation of marriage.

The Church still has a profound influence not only spiritually, but in the political arena as well. This has sparked debate about the traditional role of the Church and whether or not its close alliance with wealthy Conservatives prevents it from appealing to the majority of the people.

In comparison to Catholicism, other religions play a small role in Colombia. The mid-1980 figure for the percentage of Catholics was 97.6; the remaining 2.4% of religious adherents are Tribal Religionists (Indians), Protestants, Jews, Baha'is, Moslems, Buddhists and Hindus.

The biggest, most imposing building in Colombian towns is the Catholic church. In addition to churches, there are 161 local Baha'i spiritual assemblies, and four synagogues for the more than 10,000 Jews. Amerindian tribal religions are practiced by a number of lowland and jungle tribes including the Arhuaco, Coreguaje, Cuna, Kogua, Guajiro, Macu, Barasano and Tatuyo.

The First Communion is an important event in a person's life and for the whole family as well.

INDIVIDUAL FAITH AND PRACTICE

In 1970 a general survey found that 63% of all Catholics attended Mass at least once a week, 67% prayed daily, and only 24% did not pray at all. This represented a marked difference from results taken in 1950: only 10% of the Colombian people at that time were said to fulfill these minimum requirements of the Catholic religion. Obviously, since then there has been a resurgence of conservative worship. Though many people in urban areas only attend Mass on religious holidays, their beliefs and values remain faithful to religious teachings. Major family events such as birth and baptism, marriage and death are usually celebrated in church.

RELIGIOUS HOLIDAYS

Twelve of Colombia's 18 national holidays are religious. Many of them honor saints; Easter and Christmas are the most important. The remaining 10 religious holidays are: Epiphany (January 6); St. Joseph's Day (March 19); Maundy Thursday; Good Friday; Corpus Christi; Sts. Peter and Paul Day (June 29); Assumption Day (August 15); All Saints Day (November 1); and Immaculate Conception Day (December 8).

The Kogua Indians live in small villages in the Sierra Nevada de Santa Marta.

THE KOGUA TRIBAL RELIGION

The Kogua are Colombian Indians who live on the slopes of the Sierra Nevada de Santa Marta. This farming tribe of 5,000 treasures its ancestral lore about the laws of nature and governance of the universe. The high priest of the Kogua contemplates the skies, because true knowledge for the Kogua is the knowledge of the laws of Mother Nature. For them, living in harmony with these laws is the key to the preservation of the universe.

The high priest, or Máma, of the Kogua is responsible for watching over the universe, as well as watching over the spiritual and social order of the tribe. He knows the Kogua theory of the nine-stage creation of the universe. This knowledge, combined with the laws of nature, lets the Kogua believe that they alone hold the secret of what causes the sun to rise each morning and what determines the way things are born and mature, multiply and die.

CATHEDRALS

There are a number of notable places of worship in Colombia, most dating back to colonial days. One cathedral that is somewhat unusual is in a salt mine in Zipaquirá! It was carved from salt by the miners, and as many as 15,000 people can congregate in its immense gallery. The 75-foot high ceiling arches above an 18-ton block of salt that is the main altar.

The Church of San Francisco in Popayán has a bell that can be heard throughout the valley. In its pulpit is a gracefully carved figure of a Creole girl carrying a basket of fruit atop her head. The altarpiece carving of the Virgin of the Immaculate Conception is also breathtaking. Outside the church are simple stone carvings that stand in true contrast to the intricate carvings within.

Other beautiful churches include La Érmita (The Hermitage), which is a splendid gothic-style church located in Cali; Cartagena's cathedral, located in Plaza Bolívar, has a fortress-like exterior that was completed in the early 1600s; the Carmelita Church in Medellín is another outstanding example of Spanish colonial church architecture.

The Cathedral of Zipaquirá is located in a most unexpected place. Two hours north of Bogotá, the cathedral is built in a huge salt mine!

LANGUAGE

SPANISH IS THE DOMINANT LANGUAGE in Colombia, and it is the official language also. Colombians take pride in their language usage and are said to preserve the purest Spanish in Latin America.

Though there is remarkable ethnic diversity in the country, only about 4% of the population speaks a native Indian language. And of those people, many speak Spanish also.

Regional accents differentiate the speech of Colombians of different zones, and English is the only language spoken by the natives on San Andrés and Providencia islands. The most distinguishable accent is that of Caribbean coastal speech, where the spoken Spanish is closer to that in the Dominican Republic or Cuba than to that of Bogotá, Bucaramanga or Medellín.

Left: **Most big cities have numerous public telephones located conveniently so that people can communicate with each other faster.**

Opposite: **Local newspapers are all in Spanish, the official language of Colombia.**

THE SPANISH ALPHABET

The Spanish alphabet consists of 28 letters: **a**, **b**, **c**, **ch**, **d**, **e**, **f**, **g**, **h**, **i**, **j**, **l**, **ll**, **m**, **n**, **ñ**, **o**, **p**, **q**, **r**, **rr**, **s**, **t**, **u**, **v**, **x**, **y**, and **z**. The letters **k** and **w** do not appear in the Spanish alphabet, and they are found only in foreign words that have become part of the Spanish vocabulary. The **k** sound is represented in Spanish by **c** before **a**, **o**, and **u**, or by **qu** before **e** and **i**.

Unlike in English, each Spanish vowel has one fundamental sound:

a   as in "mama"
e   as in "they"
i   as in "police"
o   as in "low"
u   as in "rude"

Many of the consonants have the same approximate sound as in English, though a linguist would see these differences as significant. Very noticeable distinctions are:

1. **b** and **v** are pronounced identically.
2. **d**, when it is within a word, is pronounced like the English **th** in "then."
3. **s** has two sounds: it is pronounced like the **s** in "rose" when it follows **b**, **v**, **d**, **m**, **n**, **l**, **g**, **r**; otherwise it sounds like the **s** in "son."
4. **ll**, which is a symbol representing one sound, is a blend of **l** and **y**, as in "call you," or it is often simply pronounced like **y**, as in "yore."
5. **h** is not pronounced in Spanish.
6. **j** has no exact English equivalent; a throaty **h** sound is the closest English comparison; this would also be the sound for **g** before **e** and **i**.
7. **r**, within a word, is a flapped sound like the **tt** in "kitty."
8. **rr** within a word is similar to the **r** sound described above; however it is trilled.

NON-VERBAL BEHAVIOR AND GESTURES

There are not many differences in the gestures and non-verbal behavior of Colombians and North Americans, but there are a few worth mentioning.

Colombians gesture for people to come toward them in a manner that is similar to the North American wave, with the palm facing out. Also, when demonstrating a child's height, Colombians hold the hand as though it were behind the head rather than above it. "Body language" taboos in Colombia include entertaining a visitor barefoot, putting one's feet up on a desk or chair, or slouching down in a chair!

Colombians hold their hand palm outward to indicate a child's height.

Generally, Colombians living away from the coast are quite formal, and rarely raise their voices when expressing feelings or ideas, and they seldom use excited gestures. Because of their formality, anger is not often expressed directly. Instead, giving a slow response to an unwelcome question or pretending not to hear an unpopular request would be typical actions of Colombian anger.

Because of this formality, foreigners often perceive Colombians as distant or cold. Colombians regard negative responses as potentially offensive or painful, and therefore avoid giving them. For example, if a person were responding to an invitation and did not plan to attend, the response might be, "We're delighted to be invited and we'll try to come." Cultures that value directness may find this frustrating or dishonest; however, it is a matter of being considerate for Colombians.

GREETINGS

Greetings are an important part of Colombian etiquette. A verbal greeting is almost always accompanied by a handshake at the very least. Men shake hands with both women and men. Women sometimes shake hands with other women; however, they frequently shake hands by simultaneously grasping each other's right forearm. If they are close friends, they often kiss one another on the cheek. Relatives or close male friends may hug. The ritual continues by polite questioning about the well-being of family members and only then, after some small talk, is it appropriate to discuss business.

It is customary to have a short polite conversation before talking about business. To plunge straight into a business discussion would indicate a lack of social graces.

There are also procedures to follow when entering a group: everyone must be greeted, at the very least with eye and verbal contact—preferably with a handshake. It is also essential for Colombians to say goodbye to all in the group as they exit.

FORMS OF ADDRESS

When addressing a person, Colombians can use the familiar *tú* or the formal *usted* (both mean "you"); however, there are no set guidelines. Among social equals, *usted* is used, but it changes to *tú* as the people get to know one another better. Persons of higher social status or those who are given respect because of age may request others to use *tú*, but the person of lower status may feel uncomfortable using the intimate form. It is clearly not a very simple matter!

Use of first names is equated with using *tú*; before acquaintances have reached a certain familiarity, most will use Señor and Señora when addressing someone.

NEWSPAPERS

Colombia has a free press, and the leading newspapers contain a wide range of international and national news, criticism and commentary, and special features.

Newspapers have always been the major source for an accurate picture of the general state of Colombia and a vehicle for political debate. The press has been a part of Colombia's culture since 1791 when the first colonial newspaper, *Papel Periódico de la Ciudad de Santa Fe de Bogotá*, was founded.

There is a close relation between the government and the press, despite the strong belief in a free press by journalists. For example, the two leading newspapers in Bogotá, *El Tiempo* and *El Espectador,* are identified with the Liberals, and two others, *La República* and *El Siglo,* support the Conservative Party. The most influential conservative paper in the country is *El Colombiano*, which is published in Medellín.

There has always been a strong bias toward the truth of the printed word among Colombians; television and radio communications have been regulated by the government throughout the years. As a result, in this class-conscious nation, literacy has had a certain prestige which can be appreciated in the Colombian joke, "The country has two kinds of people, those with 'culture' and those with transistor radios."

Those interested in a more international slant to the news can buy the *Miami Herald* in and around Bogotá, and *The New York Times* and *The Wall Street Journal* at bookstores and newsstands in major cities.

Colombia has a long history of the press. Newsstands carry local as well as international papers and magazines.

THE ARTS

COLOMBIANS HAVE ALWAYS taken great pride in their cultural achievements, and in fact, Bogotá has been called the "Athens of Latin America" in reference to their appreciation of the arts. It is said with great pride that there are more bookstores lining the streets of the capital city than restaurants or cafés, and that more poets have become presidents than have generals!

The regionalism that is caused by Colombia's extreme geographical contrasts has also had an impact on the cultural and artistic arena: Bogotá is best known for its literature and poetry, the Caribbean coast is famed for its songs and dances, and the people of Cali and Medellín focus their creative energies into industrial ventures. Perhaps the only area of expression that is shared by all of Colombia's inhabitants is the religious festivals and rituals of the Roman Catholic Church.

Left: **Pottery is an ancient craft which is carried on today with little change in technique.**

Opposite: **This modern sculpture seems to reach up to the sky, just like the spire of the Manizales Cathedral to the left.**

One example of tribal art: Cuna Indians making a necklace out of monkey's teeth. Local appreciation of native arts started only in the 20th century.

HISTORICAL BACKGROUND

Colombia's artistic and literary presence falls into three periods: pre-Hispanic, colonial (when Colombia existed as a Spanish colony) and republican (after independence from Spain). While there was an obvious transition from the first to the second era, the change from the colonial period to the republican period was much more gradual.

The *conquistadors* destroyed any primitive Indian artistic expression they encountered when they arrived in Colombia and they insisted that all such expression be similar to what was popular in Spain. The dislike for Indian art was evident in paintings and religious sculpture of the colonial period, though some churches built during that time contain native Indian carvings. Generally, though, artistic works of the period were quite reminiscent of the Spanish style.

As the desire for independence grew, the Creoles (persons of Spanish descent who were born in the New World) rejected everything that connected them with Spain, including artistic motifs. However, much of their inspiration was based on the contemporary artistic modes of other European countries, especially France.

It was only at the beginning of the 20th century that Colombians gained a true appreciation of their indigenous artistic heritage, and what had been a mere acknowledgment of Indian monuments and colonial paintings grew into a great source of pride and a basis for modern Colombian art forms.

Beautiful gold treasures crafted by the ancient Indians reveal a great mastery of metalworking techniques.

CHRONICLING THE TIMES

Gonzalo Jiménez de Quesada introduced the chronicle, or picaresque, form into the New World. A picaresque story consists of a series of episodes or incidents from a main character's life. These are arranged in chronological order, but they are not woven into a tight plot. The picaresque novel originated in Spain; the term derives from the Spanish word *pícaro*, which means "rogue," because the principal character is usually dishonest or unscrupulous.

A couple of decades after Jiménez de Quesada's death, Juan Rodriquez Freile (1566–1640), who fought the Indians for years before settling down near Bogotá, wrote the first widely-read picaresque of the conquest and settlement of Nueva Granada, which he called *El Carnero* (The Butcher). The earliest example of a Spanish picaresque novel was *Lazaro de Tormes*, written in 1553.

The monument of "The Old Shoes" lies by the roadside in Cartagena in memory of local poet Luis Carlos Lopez.

LITERATURE

The Spanish contribution to the Colombian arts scene is most valuable in language and literature, dating back to Gonzalo Jiménez de Quesada, who was a lawyer and a scholar as well as an explorer. Colombia's first pieces of national literature came from the historical and descriptive writings of this *conquistador*. Other leaders, such as Simon Bolívar, Camilo Torres, Antonio Nariño and Francisco de Paula Santander, were also gifted writers and students of philosophy and the historical events of the day in Europe and America.

The 17th century was considered the baroque period in Latin American literature; the writing was exaggerated, flowery and not particularly notable. Neither did the following century produce celebrated works, which was perhaps a reflection of the literary state in Spain. The 19th century, however, marked the beginning of significant literary times. *Tertulias*, or literary salons, cropped up during this time, where patriots discussed forbidden books that had been smuggled into the colony.

This was the Romantic period, and poetry was the dominant literary form; the works dealt with love, patriotism, nature and religion. A major Colombian religious poet of this time was José Eusebio Caro. Character development and a variety of metrical forms marked his poetic works. So much creative energy was put into poetry during the 19th century that few outstanding novels were written during this time.

At the end of the 19th century, Colombian poets and authors formed a new literary movement called *modernismo.* This was Latin America's first original contribution to world literature, and famous literary figures from the modernist movement were José Asunción Silva and Guillermo Valencia.

Twentieth century literature focused on realistic social commentary in the form of regional novels. Tomás Carrasquilla wrote a novel about the mountain people of Antioquia; José Eustacio Riviera penned *La Vorágine* (The Vortex), which dealt with life in the Amazon. The violence in Colombia in the 1950s and 1960s also inspired significant works.

The 1960s brought a new literary age, with Gabriel García Márquez emerging as a leader. His novel, *One Hundred Years of Solitude*, was one of the most widely read novels in the Spanish language since the Second World War. Many novelists have imitated his style, emphasizing social problems and the government's inability to solve them. García Márquez received the 1982 Nobel Prize for Literature for his novels and short stories, which have been translated into many of the world's languages. *Love in the Time of Cholera* is his most recent best-selling work.

"Márquez has insights and sympathies which he can project with the intensity of a reflecting mirror in a bright sun."
— *New Statesman*

ART

Visual art also followed Spanish trends in technique and theme, and it received little attention until the 19th century, when the *costumbrista* movement began. This genre was concerned with the description of customs, manners and lifestyles. Rámon Torres Méndez is the best known artist of this era; his *Cuadros de Costumbres* (Pictures of Customs) series of paintings is almost a visual guide to life at the end of the 19th century. The *costumbrista* period was followed by one of great interest in impressionism and realism, inspired by the French movement.

Colombian artists of the 20th century introduced progressive works that followed international trends, and Alejandro Obregón emerged as

At Cali's Cañas Gordas Hacienda, an art class becomes an enjoyable outdoor experience.

REACHING OUT TO THE PEOPLE THROUGH ART

Roldanillo is a rural town of 50,000 inhabitants that is more than 400 years old. Throughout its lengthy history, most of its native sons have lived by farming and cattle raising—except for Omar Rayo, an artist of world renown and the force behind Roldanillo's imaginative Rayo Museum for Latin American Prints and Drawings.

Nearly hidden in the center of the peaceful and traditional town, the museum is a strikingly beautiful collection of eight one-room spaces that are naturally lit by glass domed ceilings. The museum is devoted to works on paper, not only because Rayo is known for his prints, but because it is the only one of its kind in Latin America.

Rayo has been living in New York in self-exile since 1960, but his commitment to his birthplace inspired him to return and share his art. It is not, however, merely an exhibition of his works; it is a workshop-museum where silk-screen, lithography, photography and photoengraving are also taught. Other artists exhibit at the Rayo Museum, but they teach and create there as well.

In conjunction with the museum, there is also an exhibit on the highway that leads from Cali to Roldanillo that displays works on billboards by 19 artists, among them Fernando Botero and Mario Toral. The highway museum, called Arte Vial, brings art to all of the people, regardless of whether they enter a museum, and it is the hope of Rayo that the rural young will now have the opportunity to become increasingly caught up in the beauty of modern art through Arte Vial and the Rayo Museum.

an important name in the modern art movement. He is considered by some art critics to be the best living artist in Colombia. Both he and Fernando Botero are world renowned modern artists.

In addition, several women have distinguished themselves for their contributions to modern art. Judith Márquez Montoya has received recognition for her many series of canvases of similar themes. Ana Mercedes de Hoyos has progressed from a "pop" style of the early 1970s to surrealism to exacting treatments of common objects such as windows and doors.

In modern times many Colombian artists have been as at home in New York and Paris, as in Bogotá.

ARCHITECTURE

Colombia's colonial architecture was consistent with Spanish styles and varied according to the climate in which it was being developed and according to the province from which the colonists originated. Fine colonial architecture can be seen in Santa Marta, Cartagena, Bogotá, Tunja and Popayán.

Ultramodern buildings are being constructed in Colombian cities all the time. In Bogotá, wide boulevards with tall glass skyscrapers create a magnificent contrast to the breathtaking colonial section. Many modern architects have studied with masterful architects of Europe and the United States, and architecture has become a very prestigious field. Works of particular merit include The Bank of Bogotá, Cartagena's baseball stadium and the Angél Arango Library.

Modern architecture is consistent with Medellín's evolution as a center of technology.

PERFORMING AND FOLK ARTS

Colombia's music and dance are very distinctive. Blacks and Indians have had a strong influence on music in the coastal regions. African-Colombian rhythms such as *fandangos, porros* and *mapales* have gained attention outside the country.

DANCING Folk dancing ranges from the exciting rhythmic steps of the coastal people to the *bambuco*, which resembles a waltz with a slightly quicker tempo. The *bambuco*, which is the national dance, is performed by couples. The *salsa* is a lively dance in which everyone whirls to trumpets and *maracas*. The *cumbia* is an Afro-Colombian rhythm that makes all listeners start tapping their feet.

Although traditional folk dancing is very popular, more progressive forms of bodily expression have emerged, such as the Barrio Ballet.

MUSIC In the Popayán region two types of traditional music, the *murga* and the *chirimia,* prevail. The *murga* is performed by wandering bands of musicians playing *tiples*, *bandolas*, guitars, mandolins and accordions. *Chirimias* are groups that perform music that is characteristic of the Indians of the lower Andes.

Instruments that are typically involved in Colombian music-making are the *flauta*, which is an Indian flute; the *tiple*, a many stringed guitar-like instrument; and the *raspa*, which is made from a gourd and played like a washboard.

The *cumbia* is a lively dance accompanied by Afro-Colombian music.

Though folk music is the dominant type of music in Colombia, classical music is also enjoyed. Bogotá is home to the National Symphony Orchestra and a National Conservatory which was founded in 1882. Concerts and operas are presented in Bogotá's Colon Theater.

DRAMA There is a long-standing dramatic tradition in Colombia; the first theater was established in the late 1700s. José Fernández Madrid (1789–1830) is considered the founder of the national theater because he is the first Colombian dramatist to write about the New World. Currently, drama is a thriving art, with numerous theaters throughout the country.

The guitar is a popular instrument of accompaniment when patrons in a bar break into impromptu singing.

LEISURE

ONCE AGAIN, the varied landscape of Colombia influences the choices for outdoor activities and provides a great assortment of things to do.

WATER SPORTS   Water sports are quite popular; fishing for marlin, tarpon, dolphin, tuna and sailfish is an enjoyable pursuit all year long, and international fishing competitions are held in Barranquilla in the months of May and November. The coast is a great place to surf. Swimming, water skiing, scuba-diving and snorkelling are exciting diversions in the inlets and bays of the Pacific. The Rosario Islands off Cartagena are a favorite place for skin-diving, but only by the very daring, because sharks and barracuda frequent the clear waters!

Left: **In Cartagena, a leisurely day at the Bocagrande Beach is enjoyed by many.**

Opposite: **As in the rest of South America, soccer is the king of sports that can draw thousands of enthusiastic spectators to the stadiums.**

MOUNTAINEERING Scaling the many mountains has become a popular pastime in recent years, as have cycling and hiking. The Sierra Nevada, approximately 30 miles from Santa Marta, provides one of the most exciting mountain climbing experiences that can be had. The peaks of the Sierra Nevada are nearly 19,000 feet.

HUNTING Game hunting has long been a favored sport of the wealthy. With tapirs, deer and boar roaming in the wilderness, and organized safaris in the *llanos* of the Amazon basin, there is much to keep the avid hunter busy.

Skiing is an exhilarating experience on the slopes of the Nevado del Ruiz.

SPORTS

In the last 20 years Colombians have shown a growing interest in sports. As in most Latin American countries, soccer is far and away the favorite sport, though baseball and basketball have their share of devotees. There is a women's basketball league made up of teams representing the various departments (states) of the country. Also, Colombian players regularly participate in international table tennis competitions.

There is much greater access to recreational facilities in the cities than in rural areas, and in places like Bogotá, for example, there are countless opportunities for spectator and competitor alike. Local auto racing events are held on Sundays and holidays; boxing tournaments are held in Bogotá's Coliseo El Salitre. Golf, tennis, bowling and skiing are popular, but are generally only available to the very wealthy.

City dwellers are more aware that sports are good for health. Regular exercising, such as aerobics, has a beneficial impact on the level of fitness.

LA CORRIDA

Bullfighting is so popular that there are two bullfighters' unions and most cities have *plazas de toros* (bullfighting rings). There are bullfights all year round, but the most exciting ones are in February and December, when visiting *toreros* (bullfighters) come in for the international festivals.

Though bullfighting is a dangerous profession, it is a matter of grace, courage and skill for the *matador* (the bullfighter who kills the bull).

The bulls are creatures bred specifically for fighting. They are aggressive, obstinate and extremely strong.

Bullfights take place on Thursday and Sunday afternoons. In a typical program three *matadors* fight two bulls each. Before the contest, they parade around the arena in their beautifully hand-tailored suits, called *trajes de luces* (suits of lights). The *matadors* head the procession armed with swords, and they are followed by six-man teams who assist them.

La Corrida

The crowds are screaming at nearly fever-pitch by the time the parade is finished, and then the bullfight begins. A trumpet sounds, the bull pen opens and the bull charges out into the ring.

Members of the team begin to taunt the bull so that the *matador* can observe its movements. He begins with some moves with the cape, called passes, which are done without the *matador* even moving his feet! Then the *picadors* harass the bull by prodding its shoulders with lances, weakening its neck muscles. They are followed by the *banderilleros*, who also insert darts into the bull's neck. Attached to the darts are ribbons, which are included for their colorful effect.

Although bullfighting is a cruel sport condemned by animal lovers, it still draws excited crowds to bullrings in all Spanish speaking countries.

The third and final act consists of the *matador* re-entering the ring, whereupon he does some maneuvers that prepare the bull for the kill by means of some passes. Well executed passes bring cheers of "Olé!" from the crowd. After what the *matador* feels is the correct number of passes, he proceeds to the kill, which is done with a thrust of the sword.

The most admired method is called the *recibiendo*. It is a perfectly executed thrust between the horns that makes the bull fall dead. This maneuver is quite dangerous, for the *matador* must stand perfectly still while the enraged animal lunges toward him. The more common procedure is the *volapié*, which allows the *matador* to dodge the charging bull and deliver the fatal blow between the shoulder blades.

This is a dangerous sport, for a simple movement of the bull's horns can gore the *matador*. If the *matador* has performed successfully, the bull dies immediately and the crowd cheers. A mere wounding of the bull provokes a screaming fury from the crowd!

COCKFIGHTING

Cockfighting is a very popular sport. Trained gamecocks are put beak to beak on a stage or in a pit and are let loose to fight one another. The gamecocks are usually fitted with razor-sharp spurs; the competition goes on until one is killed, can no longer fight or refuses to fight. Three types of cockfights are held: the single

battle, in which two cocks fight; the main battle, in which cocks are paired and play an elimination tournament; and the battle royal, in which several cocks fight one another until only one is left standing.

Cockfighting is one of the many games on which Colombians like to bet.

BETTING

An activity that is very popular among both rich and poor is gambling on games of chance. Estimates indicate that Colombians spend as much as 25% of their regular income on gambling, regardless of how small or large that income is.

Lotteries are prevalent throughout the country, and they are thought to serve an important social function, because the country's welfare program and hospitals receive a generous portion of the profits.

In addition to this government-sponsored activity, there are numerous gambling casinos and horse racing tracks, and there is always considerable wagering on other sporting events.

One of the traditional games in Colombia is *tejo* which gives rise to a lot of noise and excitement on Sundays.

TEJO

Tejo is a traditional game that is similar to horseshoe pitching; nearly every Colombian town has a *tejo* court. Two mounds of dirt are built around pipes that are set about 40 feet apart. The tops of the pipes are loaded with small amounts of gunpowder (*mecha*) and are level with the tops of the mounds of dirt. The *tejo*, which is a smooth round piece of metal or stone, is thrown at the top of the mound, and the object of the game is to explode the *mecha*.

Tejo experts reside throughout the countryside, and on Sundays after church or in the afternoons on market days, the sound of exploding *mechas* provides much excitement and commotion.

SPORTS IN RURAL AREAS

In rural areas, there are sports clubs and leagues that are affiliated with the local churches or sponsored by municipalities. Chess, bicycle races, soccer, volleyball, and *tejo* are the activities that are most likely to occupy the free time of the people of the countryside.

As Colombians grow more affluent, shopping becomes a pleasure. All the cities have large shopping malls with a variety of goods.

SHOPPING

A favorite leisure-time activity among urban Colombians is shopping. There are national department stores that carry a full array of consumer items, as well as several Sears stores. Bogotá is home to Unicentro, which is the largest shopping mall in Colombia and the 10th largest in the world. There are several other smaller malls in the northern part of the city. Avid shoppers can find almost anything in Unicentro Bogotá, including pre-Columbian artifacts! A smaller Unicentro and two other lovely malls are located in Cali, and Medellín and Barranquilla have ample shopping facilities.

GETTING AWAY

Colombian city dwellers love to escape from the hustle and bustle of city life and take off for the countryside. Many people make a practice of taking an extra-long weekend when a holiday falls on a Tuesday or Thursday. They call these long weekends *puentes*, or bridges. Lake Guatavita, which is northeast of Bogotá, is a favorite spot for *puentes*. The Caribbean coast is also a restful resort area that Colombians like to visit at vacation time because of its beautiful beaches.

One favorite leisure activity for city dwellers is to go out to the countryside. Many Cali residents like to take a Sunday dip in the Rio Panle.

FESTIVALS

THE WORD "FIESTA" brings to mind a whimsical celebration with laughter, dancing, music and merriment. There may be much ringing of church bells and even fireworks. However, there is usually a serious reason behind the activities, and often a somber tone pervades the celebration of these special events.

Opposite: **A joyous atmosphere pervades the music festival at Ginebra. Locals take the opportunity to ride in horse-drawn carriages or to sell their wares.**

FIESTA Fiestas are held to commemorate tribal, civic and religious milestones. Tribal fiestas can mark the harvest, a child's first haircut or a seasonal happening, such as the beginning of the rainy season. Civic festivities usually include speeches, parades and sometimes athletic competitions. Religious fiestas are usually the most numerous and most colorful.

While there is a serious and somber background to each feast day, the purpose behind the celebration is both worship and entertainment. Generally, a rural fiesta will emphasize the worship aspect. Special Masses mark the

day along with a procession that features a holy image and great ceremony. Often a market day will be coordinated with the activities so vendors can display their wares for a large crowd.

Above: **In Cali, a cavalcade along the main streets of the town usually opens the annual fair.**

The allegorical float procession on Epiphany Day is a most colorful event in Túquerres.

FERIAS

Fiestas that are associated with a religious pilgrimage and that last a week or more are called *ferias*. Dancing is usually part of the religious fiesta. Ritual dances may be performed in the courtyard of the church or in the church proper, and women generally do not take part in them. A ritual dance is a serious matter that usually includes a dramatization and dialogue for a specific purpose such as honoring a saint. A folk dance, on the other hand, is a social matter whose main purpose is entertainment, and can be performed by both men and women, young and old.

Some of the most colorful festivals are those of indigenous tribes and Caribbean blacks. Among Andean tribes, as a result of missionary efforts, there has been a blending of Christian saints and pagan gods. For example, many Indians do not see much difference between the Mama (Mother

Nature) and the Virgin Mary. Coastal blacks have combined the rituals and beliefs of their native lands with the Christianity they have embraced as Colombians.

Regardless of whether the celebration is strictly Christian, an Indian ritual or a hodgepodge of black, Christian and pagan ceremonies, the fiesta is an opportunity to bring zest and color into lives that are often a simple and trying struggle. The fiesta is a wonderful contrast to the everyday sameness of poverty and labor. Because it occurs yearly, it is a magical time for all to anticipate; it becomes a project for all in the community to plan and revel in once spirited times begin.

The festival of Colombia's national patron, the Virgin Mary of the Rosary of Chinquinquira, is one of the most famous in the Americas.

SAN ISIDRO

April marks the end of the dry season, and so on April 4, the image of San Isidro (St. Isadore the Farmer), who is responsible for bringing the rains, is carried throughout the town of Río Frío. All the townspeople follow his image and chant his praises.

In their chanting, the local farmers explain the need for rain, and optimally, San Isidro will cooperate by bringing the first shower before the celebration is completed. So as not to demand too much of the saint, the parade is slow and drawn out—every two steps a participant takes are followed by one step backward!

If San Isidro has not cooperated after several processions through the town, the tone of the chanting changes from praise to scolding. As the hours pass, the yelling becomes progressively more belligerent until the townspeople can be heard screaming profanities! Should there be no change in the skies, San Isidro is put away until the next April, when the worshipers will hope for better results.

DIA DE NEGRITOS/FIESTA DE LOS BLANQUITOS

The *chirimias*, groups of strolling musicians, take to the streets to create an air of fanfare during the carnival of the blacks and the whites.

In Popayán during the first week of January there is a Mardi Gras atmosphere to celebrate the end of the Christmas season. January 5 is the Día de Negritos (Day of the Black Ones) and the next day is the Fiesta de los Blanquitos (Festival of the White Ones). Many people think that the color references are to the biblical Three Wise Men, who reached their destination on the sixth day of the month. However, the names refer to the day's activities.

On the morning of the Día de Negritos, boys with shoe polish chase the girls of the community and decorate them with their blackened hands; as the day progresses, older boys chase after older girls, and by the time evening falls, no one is safe from the marauding boys. The present-day frivolity derives from more dignified earlier practices.

In days of old, gentlemen paraded beneath ladies' balconies, and when the ladies came to the door, the men were allowed to paint a spot on the ladies' cheek or forehead. The festivities have grown more rowdy over the years, and today a great many people stay indoors to avoid the fracas.

There are still street parades in the afternoon with people in masquerade and the *chirimias*, or strolling groups, playing the latest Colombian

bambucos on primitive instruments. At the main square, the *tasajo*, or distribution of foods donated by rich farmowners, takes place. When night falls, the celebrations continue at a social club or in private homes, with dancing and partying till dawn.

On the following morning, the focus is on white. Boys chase girls in the streets with white flour. Young people ride around the town tossing the white powder on everyone they see. Then, people on balconies pour water on the flour-coated pedestrians, until everyone is laden with a sticky mixture. There is much merrymaking and drinking, while older Colombians remember the beauty of the religious activities that the day formerly celebrated.

Masquerades add to the Mardi Gras atmosphere during the Fiesta de los Blanquitos.

The word "carnival" evokes a vision of glittering costumes and unending merrymaking. Colombian carnivals are more subdued than in other parts of South America; but still there is much dancing in the street.

Music, on its own or as accompaniment, is an important element of carnivals all over the world.

CARNIVAL

The word "Carnival" comes from the Latin, *carne vale* (farewell to flesh) which aptly says what happens in the last days before Lent. The philosophy behind the carousing is that giving in to one's desires beforehand will make it easier to realize the upcoming religious experiences.

The whole of Colombia participates in the festivities of Carnival; however, the celebration in Barranquilla is most famous. The city begins preparing for Carnival just after Christmas, and the two months preceding Lent are filled with masquerades and dancing in the public square.

Several ritual dances are performed during Carnival: the *maestranza* is a comical dance with men dressed as women. The *danza de los pájaros* is also danced by men wearing colorful costumes representing plumage and masks with beaks.

The *coyongos* is a ritual dance-drama. A *coyongo* is a large aquatic fishing bird, and in this dance, several bird-men circle around a man dressed as a fish who tries to evade the birds that are closing in.

Above: Beauty contests are organized in every town, but the most important one takes place in Cartagena on the town's Independence Day.

Opposite: Great imagination and ingenuity are deployed by the villagers of Túquerres in the design of their costumes for the parade on the afternoon of the Fiesta de los Blanquitos.

INDEPENDENCE OF CARTAGENA

This annual carnival takes place on the November 11 anniversary of the Declaration of Independence. The old city surrounded by walls has a four-day celebration featuring thousands of people in costume dancing in the streets to the sound of *maracas* and drums. There are parades, floral displays and frenzied excitement caused by fireworks called *buscapies* (feet searchers), which send crowds reeling as the firecrackers bounce along the streets.

People dance throughout the night and wander in the streets to the music of guitars, *maracas* and drums. The festivities culminate with the National Beauty Contest, which selects the young woman who will represent Colombia in international beauty contests.

CALENDAR OF FESTIVALS

January	New Year's Day Epiphany Day	June	Sts. Peter and Paul Day
February	Candlemas	July	Independence Day
March	St. Joseph's Day	August	Battle of Boyacá Feast of the Assumption
March/April	Maundy Thursday Good Friday Holy Saturday Easter	October	Columbus Day
		November	All Saints Day Independence of Cartagena
May	Labor Day Ascension Day	December	Feast of the Immaculate Conception Christmas
June	Corpus Christi		

FOOD

KITCHENS IN RURAL HOMES of poor families are quite simple, for there is no refrigeration, electricity or running water in the home. There may be a small gas stove with one or two burners, but all water for drinking and cooking must be drawn from a well. It is not unusual for a woman of a rural home to kill, pluck and prepare a chicken as a routine part of preparing dinner.

Kitchens in larger cities are just considered rooms in which the maid prepares the meals; the dining room is where the family eats all three meals of the day. Colombian homes do not have eat-in kitchens or breakfast nooks like those found in North America. The kitchen is actually off-limits for most family members. There is, of course, running water, but even in many upper-middle class families there may not be modern electrical appliances such as toasters, freezers and automatic ovens. With less than up-to-date appliances, it is no wonder that a maid is considered a vital member for the middle and upper-class household.

Colombians have a strong cultural bias against standing water, and as a result, dishes are washed in running water; they are never soaked. Maids seldom cap the drain in the sink or collect water in a dishpan to clean up after a meal. Rather, they keep the water running, scrape everything off the dish, and then wash it with a soapy sponge before rinsing it under the running faucet.

Opposite: **Housewives buy live chickens at the market and bring them home to slaughter and pluck.**

Below: **In Jurumbira, pounding the rice is a daily activity. Chickens crowd round the mortar to peck at the grains which fall to the ground.**

In well-to-do city households, the señora is in charge of the cooking while her maids wash the dishes and unpack the groceries.

Hot water heaters are also not common in Colombia. In rural areas, water for cooking, bathing and washing clothes is boiled in a large pot over the fire or gas stove. City dwellers have water heaters that must be lit. Because gas is costly, some families have the maid light the water heater each morning so that there is sufficient water for the family to shower, and it is routinely turned off after breakfast.

As a result, dishes are washed in cold water. It is customary to leave the water running for long periods of time. It also makes perfect sense not to soak the dishes, for dirty dishes bathed in cold water would certainly lead to an unsavory mess!

THE NATIONAL DRINK

There are four types of Colombian coffee: *caturra*, *maragojipe*, *pajarito* and *borbón*. These are grown under banana trees which shade them from the sunlight. Because only the ripest beans can be harvested, they must be hand-picked and dried on racks for several days. In some villages it is the job of the children to turn the beans so that both sides are thoroughly dried.

Supremo is the highest grade of bean; *extra* is a lower grade. *Excelso* is a blend of the high and lower-grade beans. This blend of coffee is exported to the United States in larger quantities than any other coffee.

In Colombia, coffee is served with every meal. A small cup of black coffee is called a *tinto*, and it often contains as much sugar as coffee. Coffee with milk is known as *café perico*; *café con leche* is a cup of warm milk with coffee added.

There are no coffee breaks in Colombian offices, because people drink so much coffee that they would never be off break. Instead, a woman travels from desk to desk and dispenses *tintos*. Average coffee consumption for a Colombian is 20 cups per day.

Right: **A wide range of food and household items are available at the supermarkets in the main cities.**

Opposite top: **The** *tienda* **is a small grocery shop which also serves as a convenient meeting place for villagers.**

Opposite bottom: **The Magdalena valley is a rich agricultural region. Thus a variety of tropical fruits are on display at every roadside stall.**

FOOD SHOPPING

Shopping in the major cities of Colombia is very similar to that in North America. The large supermarket chains are Cafam, Carulla, Fortuna, Ley, and Olimpica. Almost any item can be found in the city, but many foods are imported and are only available in delicatessens and specialty stores.

A wide variety of fruits and vegetables is available throughout the year; they are usually moderately priced, but fruits that are imported from North America like pears, apples and plums can be costly. Meats are a bit less expensive than in the United States, and because animals are grass-fed, the meats are usually leaner. The taste also is somewhat different from that in North America because the meat is not aged.

In small towns or in the neighborhood meat market, there may be no refrigeration. So, after the pork or beef is brought directly from the slaughterhouse, a red flag is hung out so the customers know that the meat has come in. The meat is purchased quickly and taken home to be prepared for the next meal.

Rural villages usually have a small store, or *tienda*, where people buy goods such as cigarettes, food, beer and other assorted items. The *tienda* is also a social center where villagers come to visit and share gossip with each other. It may consist of no more than one room, perhaps attached to the owner's house, with a counter where employees gather merchandise for the customers. *Tiendas* are open in the evenings and are particularly busy on weekends. In towns and villages where there is more than one *tienda*, customers choose the *tienda* at which to shop according to political preferences, with Conservatives shopping at one, and Liberals at the other.

On market days, the food stalls sell a variety of local dishes. Notice that the left hand is always above the table.

MEALTIMES

Breakfast, lunch and dinner are the traditional meals. The morning meal is not a family meal in Colombia. Everyone eats according to the needs of his or her personal schedule. The father, who may have to leave for work as early as 7 a.m., will eat breakfast earliest. Children's breakfast time depends on whether they have to go to school and what time the school bus will be picking them up. Typical breakfast foods include juice, fruit, jam, and, of course, coffee.

Lunch, on the other hand, is the most important meal for the family, and the father returns home for it. This may be his only opportunity to spend time with young children since he may not return home in the evening before their bedtime. Lunch is eaten around 12:30 or 1 p.m. and may last till as late as 2:30 p.m. Soup, rice, meat with vegetables and dessert are the typical courses for the midday meal.

The evening meal, eaten at around 7 p.m., can consist of the same fare as lunch, but soup is usually not served.

TABLE MANNERS

Table manners in the Colombian home are similar to those in the homes of their northern neighbors. However, Colombians feel that the left hand should be visible and above the table.

Food is served on the individual's plate, and a small amount is left at the end of the meal to show that it was plentiful. Silverware placed horizontally across the plate indicates that a person has finished.

Colombians are quite formal at mealtimes. Although breakfast is not a family meal, pajamas or bathrobes and slippers are not permissible. At lunch and dinner all family members are expected to be dressed as though they were ready to go out, which may include a jacket or sweater for women and a jacket and tie for men.

HIGH ALTITUDE COOKING

In Medellín, Bogotá and any other region higher than 5,000 feet above sea level, cooks must practice high altitude cooking. Because air has less pressure at higher altitudes, recipes must be modified or the quality of the food being cooked is impaired.

Foods that suffer most from changes in altitude are those that require baking or boiling and those that contain a lot of sugar. Water boils at a higher temperature at high altitudes, so it takes longer to prepare boiled foods. Pressure cookers are quite helpful in such cases.

Since most breads and cakes depend on yeast or baking powder for their shape and consistency, the decreased pressure makes it necessary to reduce the leavening agents so cakes and breads do not collapse. For baking in the highlands, the rule-of-thumb is to reduce baking powder, shortening and sugar slightly and increase eggs and liquid slightly.

FOODS OF COLOMBIA

Foods in Colombia are rich and highly seasoned, but not necessarily spicy. Starches are a great part of the Colombian diet, including potatoes, rice and *yuca*, which is a root. Overall, however, the Colombian menu is a mixture of Indian and Spanish traditions. What individuals eat from that menu is a reflection of economic status and regional tastes.

One popular dish throughout the country is *ajiaco*, which is a highly seasoned soup of potatoes, chicken, capers, corn and slices of avocado. Soup is served much more often and in many more varieties in Colombia than in the United States. It is even occasionally served as breakfast or as a main course. *Changua* soup is a favorite Andean breakfast. It is a blend of beef broth, milk and chopped coriander. *Sopa de pan* is a main course soup that uses bread, eggs, and cheese; it is quite filling and full of nutrients. Other popular soups are made with vegetable, plantain, which is a fruit similar to the banana, rice and potato.

Some very tasty breads are served in Colombia. *Arepa* is a simple cornbread of Indian origin. It is made of ground corn mixed with a little salt and enough water to make a stiff dough, which is toasted on a greased griddle. *Arepas* are eaten by rich and poor alike—

Beef is the most plentiful meat in Colombia, and in rural areas, it is broiled over a charcoal fire by the roadside.

118

the poor eat them because *arepas* are very economical, the rich because it is a tradition. *Mogollos* are whole wheat muffins with a raisin-flavored center which are served with dinner. *Roscones* are buns filled with guava jelly and sprinkled with sugar. *Almojábanas* are corn muffins enriched with cottage cheese.

Colombian beef is somewhat tougher than the beef in the United States, but Colombian cooks have found some wonderfully tasty ways to tenderize and prepare it. Rather than grinding the beef into hamburger meat, they slice it into tiny cubes and sauté, broil or add it to soups. The size of the cubes prevents them from becoming tough. Another zesty Colombian tenderizing method is to simmer a chunk of meat for several hours and then baste and roast it for several more.

The *arepa* is a tasty cornbread which is enjoyed by each and every Colombian.

Bananas grow in abundance in Chocó and they are used to prepare several types of dishes.

REGIONAL DELICACIES

Regional favorites have much to do with what types of vegetables and fruits grow in the area. For example, the high cool mountain valleys near Bogotá produce white potatoes in abundance, and recipes of that region make good use of that vegetable. *Papas chorreadas* are boiled potatoes, but they are covered with a flavorful sauce of coriander, cream, tomatoes, cheese and scallions.

Though the region around Bogotá is cool, the warm zones are quite close by, and the cooks of the capital city have an abundance of tropical fruits available to them. Bananas and avocados are favored ingredients; there are perhaps a dozen ways that the people of Bogotá prepare green bananas. Avocados are added to all types of salads and soups.

120

People of Indian and African descent who inhabit the jungles grow *yuca*, corn, beans and plantains, and they catch the local wildlife for meat. They eat monkeys, tapirs, and any kind of bird except parrot, which is too tough. Ants are a delicacy for rural Colombians as well as for the jungle people. The insects are caught in large quantity during mating season and are fried in oil or fat.

In the western part of the country, particularly the Cauca valley, there is also a distinctive local cuisine that makes wonderful use of the *yuca* and plantain that thrive in the warm climate. The leathery leaves of the plantains are used to wrap various recipes of corn and other ingredients for steaming and boiling. One such treat is *hallaca*, which is similar to the *tamales* of Mexico.

The Colombian *tamales* make use of plantain leaves to wrap the ingredients, instead of the cornhusk favored in Mexico.

PAPAS CHORREADAS

2 tablespoon butter
4 scallions
1/2 cup finely chopped onions
5 tomatoes, peeled, seeded and chopped
1/2 cup heavy cream

1 teaspoon coriander
1/4 teaspoon dried oregano
pinch of cumin
1/2 teaspoon salt
1 cup grated mozzarella

8 large potatoes, peeled and boiled

1. Heat butter over moderate heat in a 10-inch skillet.
2. Add scallions and onions and cook them, stirring frequently for 5 minutes, or until onions are soft and transparent.
3. Add tomatoes and cook, stirring for 5 minutes.
4. Add cream, coriander, oregano, cumin, and salt, stirring constantly.
5. Continue stirring and drop in cheese; stir until cheese melts.
6. Serve over sliced boiled potatoes.

A "restaurant" in rural areas can be nothing more than boards held by wooden poles, where the locals come for a drink and a bite.

DINING OUT

There is an exciting variety of international restaurants in the larger cities of Colombia. However, many Colombian restaurants take pride in serving dishes typical of their region. At finer restaurants, waiters are particularly polite and provide excellent service. There may be as many as three to four waiters per table to serve the diners' every need.

In less formal eateries, Colombians sometimes make a hissing sound to call a waiter or they clap their hands twice to get the attention of their server. Fast food lovers can find some of their favorites in Bogotá— Burger King, Pizza Hut and Wimpy's dot the city streets. There are also local hamburger shops in all the major cities, and *cantinas* sell snacks, tropical fruit juices and coffee.

DRINKING CUSTOMS

Colombians do not drink much liquid with meals; however, milk is served to children at mealtimes. Coffee, of course, is the national beverage, and it is consumed frequently after and between meals. Fruit juices and colas are favorite soft drinks, and they are usually highly sweetened. Colombians love sugar!

Beer is a favorite drink between meals, and in rural areas it is occasionally drunk with meals. Wine is served at dinner when there are guests, but it is not typically served at a family meal. Because Colombia produces very little wine, it must be imported and can be very expensive.

A traditional Indian alcoholic beverage is *chicha*, a potent corn liquor. The government outlawed *chicha* in 1948, but it continues to be a popular drink, especially throughout the countryside, where alcohol is an important part of community life on market days and at *tiendas*, for example.

Other favorite liquors are rum, *aguardiente* (licorice-flavored brandy), and *guarapo* (fermented brown sugar). Guests are encouraged by their hosts to have alcoholic drinks in social situations, because failure to "join the party" is seen as being snobbish.

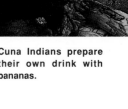

Cuna Indians prepare their own drink with bananas.

CARIBBEAN SEA

Sta Marta

Barranquilla

Cartagena

PANAMA

R. Sinú

R. Cauca

R. Magdalena

R. César

VENEZUELA

PACIFIC OCEAN

R. Atrato

Medellín

Bucaramanga

Bogotá

R. Meta

COLOMBIA

Buenaventura

Cali

R. Guaviare

R. Vaupés

R. Caguán

R. Caquetá

ECUADOR

BRAZIL

Equator

Rio Putumayo

Amazon

P E R U

N

124

Amazon D5

Barranquilla B1
Bogotá B3
Brazil D5
Bucaramanga B2
Buenaventura A3

Cali A3
Caribbean Sea A1
Cartagena B1

Ecuador A5
Equator A4

Medellín B2

Pacific Ocean A3
Panama A2
Peru B5

R. Amazon D5
R. Atrato A2
R. Caguán B4
R. Cauca B2
R. Caquetá C4
R. César B1
R. Guaviare D3
R. Magdalena B2
R. Meta C3

R. Sinú B2
R. Vaupés C4
Rio Putumayo C5

Sta Marta B1

Venezuela D2

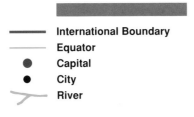

—— International Boundary
—— Equator
● Capital
● City
〜 River

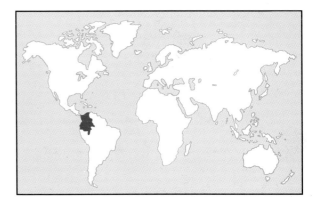

QUICK NOTES

AREA
440,000 square miles

POPULATION
31.2 million

CAPITAL
Bogotá

NATIONAL FLOWER
Cattleya orchid

NATIONAL ANTHEM
El Himno Nacional

DEPARTMENTS (STATES)
Antioquia, Atlántico, Bolívar, Boyacá, Caldas, Cauca, César, Chocó, Córdoba, Cundinamarca, Huila, La Guajira, Magdalena, Meta, Nariño, Norte de Santander, Quindío, Risaralda, Santander, Sucre, Tolima, Valle del Cauca

MAJOR RIVERS
Amazon, Atrato, Sinú, Magdalena, Orinoco

HIGHEST POINT
Sierra Nevada (19,055 feet)

MOUNTAIN RANGES
Cordillera Central, Cordillera Occidental, Cordillera Oriental, Sierra Nevada de Santa Marta

NATIONAL LANGUAGE
Spanish

MAJOR RELIGION
Roman Catholic

CURRENCY
100 centavos per peso
(US$1 = 455 pesos)

MAIN EXPORTS
Coffee, bananas, fuel oil, cotton, flowers

IMPORTANT ANNIVERSARIES
Independence Day (July 20)
Independence of Cartagena (November 11)
Battle of Boyacá (August 7)

LEADERS IN POLITICS
Simon Bolívar—first president of Gran
    Colombia
César Gaviria—current president

LEADERS IN THE ARTS
Gabriel García Márquez (writer)
Fernando Botero (artist)
Noé Léon (artist)
José Asunción Silva (poet)
Jorge Isaac (writer)

GLOSSARY

bogotano	Belonging to Bogotá; inhabitant of Bogotá.
compadrazgo	Spiritual relationship between a child's godparent and parents.
concordat	Agreement between a pope and a government for the regulation of church matters.
cordillera	Mountain range.
department	State.
feria	Festival associated with a pilgrimage.
llanos	Grassy lowlands to the north and east of the mountain ranges.
mestizo	Person of Spanish-Indian ancestry.
páramo	Cold, bleak plain.
sabana	Savannah, treeless plain.
turgurios	Slums.
vaqueros	Cowboys.

BIBLIOGRAPHY

Background Notes: Republic of Colombia, Washington, D.C.: U.S. Department of State (updated periodically.)

Holt, Pat: *Colombia Today—and Tomorrow*, Praeger, New York, 1964.

Labbe, Armand J.: *Colombia Before Columbus*, Rizzoli International Publications, Inc., New York, 1986.

MacEoin, Gary: *Colombia, Venezuela, and the Guianas*, Time, Inc., New York, 1965.

INDEX

Picture Credits

Victor Englebert, Eduardo Gil, John Maier Jr., New York Public Library, South American Pictures (Nicholas Bright, Marion Morrison, Tony Morrison), Lesley Thelander, UPI/Bettmann